Favorite Brand Name™
GIFTS FROM THE
Christmas
KITCHEN

Publications International, Ltd.

Favorite Brand Name Recipes at www.fbnr.com

Front cover photography: Sanders Studios, Inc., Chicago

Pictured on the front cover *(clockwise from top right):* Cherry Eggnog Quick Bread *(page 100)*, Cookies and Cream Cheesecake Bonbons *(page 178)*, Chocolate Reindeer *(page 122)*, Crispy Thumbprint Cookies *(page 142)*, Chocolate-Dipped Orange Logs *(page 120)*, Triple Layer Chocolate Mints *(page 176)*, Cracked Peppercorn Honey Mustard *(page 48)* and Soft Pretzels *(page 12)*.

Pictured on the back cover *(clockwise from top right):* Cranberry Cheesecake Muffins *(page 76)*, Asian Spicy Sweet Mustard and Cracked Peppercorn Honey Mustard *(page 48)* and Cranberry-Orange Snack Mix *(page 34)*.

ISBN: 0-7853-9392-7

Library of Congress Catalog Card Number: 2003101568

Manufactured in China.

8 7 6 5 4 3 2 1

Microwave Cooking: Microwave ovens vary in wattage. Use the cooking times as guidelines and check for doneness before adding more time.

Preparation/Cooking Times: Preparation times are based on the approximate amount of time required to assemble the recipe before cooking, baking, chilling or serving. These times include preparation steps such as measuring, chopping and mixing. The fact that some preparations and cooking can be done simultaneously is taken into account. Preparation of optional ingredients and serving suggestions is not included.

CONTENTS

SENSATIONAL SEASONAL SNACKS

Caramel-Cinnamon Snack Mix

2 tablespoons vegetable oil
½ cup popcorn kernels
½ teaspoon salt, divided
1½ cups packed light brown sugar
½ cup butter or margarine
½ cup corn syrup
¼ cup red hot cinnamon candies
2 cups cinnamon-flavored shaped graham crackers
1 cup red and green candy-coated chocolate pieces

1. Grease 2 large baking pans; set aside. Heat oil in large saucepan over high heat until hot. Add popcorn kernels. Cover pan. Shake pan constantly over heat until kernels no longer pop. Divide popcorn evenly between 2 large bowls. Add ¼ teaspoon salt to each bowl; toss to coat. Set aside.

2. Preheat oven to 250°F. Combine brown sugar, butter and corn syrup in heavy medium saucepan. Cook over medium heat until sugar melts, stirring constantly with wooden spoon. Bring mixture to a boil. Boil 5 minutes, stirring frequently.

3. Remove ½ of sugar mixture (about ¾ cup) from saucepan; pour over 1 portion of popcorn. Toss with lightly greased spatula until evenly coated.

4. Add red hot candies to saucepan. Stir constantly with wooden spoon until melted. Pour over remaining portion of popcorn; toss with lightly greased spatula until evenly coated.

5. Spread each portion of popcorn in even layer in separate prepared pans with lightly greased spatula.

6. Bake 1 hour, stirring every 15 minutes to prevent popcorn from sticking together. Cool completely in pans. Combine popcorn, graham crackers and chocolate pieces in large bowl. Store in airtight container at room temperature up to 1 week.   *Makes about 4 quarts*

Cheese Straws

½ cup (1 stick) butter, softened
⅛ teaspoon salt
 Dash ground red pepper
1 pound sharp Cheddar cheese, shredded, at room temperature
2 cups self-rising flour

Heat oven to 350°F. In mixer bowl, beat butter, salt and pepper until creamy. Add cheese; mix well. Gradually add flour, mixing until dough begins to form a ball. Form dough into ball with hands. Fit cookie press with small star plate; fill with dough according to manufacturer's directions. Press dough onto cookie sheets in 3-inch-long strips (or desired shapes). Bake 12 minutes, just until lightly browned. Cool completely on wire rack. Store tightly covered. *Makes about 10 dozen*

*Favorite recipe from **Southeast United Dairy Industry Association, Inc.***

Jingle Bells Chocolate Pretzels

1 cup HERSHEY'S Semi-Sweet Chocolate Chips
1 cup HERSHEY'S Premier White Chips, divided
1 tablespoon plus ½ teaspoon shortening (do not use butter, margarine, spread or oil), divided
 About 24 salted or unsalted pretzels (3×2 inches)

1. Cover tray or cookie sheet with wax paper.

2. Place chocolate chips, ⅔ cup white chips and 1 tablespoon shortening in medium microwave-safe bowl. Microwave at HIGH (100%) 1 minute; stir. Microwave at HIGH an additional 1 to 2 minutes, stirring every 30 seconds, until chips are melted when stirred.

3. Using fork, dip each pretzel into chocolate mixture; tap fork on side of bowl to remove excess chocolate. Place coated pretzels on prepared tray.

4. Place remaining ⅓ cup white chips and remaining ½ teaspoon shortening in small microwave-safe bowl. Microwave at HIGH 15 to 30 seconds or until chips are melted when stirred. Using tines of fork, drizzle chip mixture across pretzels. Refrigerate until coating is set. Store in airtight container in cool, dry place.

Makes about 24 coated pretzels

White Dipped Pretzels: Cover tray with wax paper. Place 1⅔ cups (10-ounce package) HERSHEY'S Premier White Chips and 2 tablespoons shortening (do not use butter, margarine, spread or oil) in medium microwave-safe bowl. Microwave at HIGH 1 to 2 minutes or until chips are melted when stirred. Dip pretzels as directed above. Place ¼ cup HERSHEY'S Semi-Sweet Chocolate Chips and ¼ teaspoon shortening (do not use butter, margarine, spread or oil) in small microwave-safe bowl. Microwave at HIGH 30 seconds to 1 minute or until chips are melted when stirred. Drizzle melted chocolate across pretzels, using tines of fork. Refrigerate and store as directed above.

Maple-Cinnamon Almonds

¼ **cup maple-flavored syrup**
3 **tablespoons butter**
2 **tablespoons sugar**
1½ **teaspoons ground cinnamon**
¼ **teaspoon salt**
1 **pound blanched whole almonds**
¼ **cup crystallized vanilla sugar* (optional)**

*Look for crystallized sugar where either gourmet coffees or cake decorating supplies are sold.

1. Preheat oven to 325°F. Line two 15×10×1-inch jelly-roll pans with foil.

2. Combine syrup, butter, sugar, cinnamon and salt in heavy medium saucepan. Bring to a boil over high heat, stirring frequently. Boil 30 seconds. Remove from heat; stir in almonds with wooden spoon, tossing to coat evenly.

3. Spread almond mixture in single layer in one prepared pan. Bake about 40 minutes or until almonds are crisp and dry, stirring every 15 minutes. Immediately transfer almonds to remaining prepared pan; sprinkle evenly with crystallized sugar. Cool completely. Store in airtight container at room temperature up to 1 week.
Makes about 3½ cups nuts

Note: If almonds become tacky upon storing, place on baking sheet lined with foil. Bake at 325°F 15 to 20 minutes; cool.

Take-Along Snack Mix

1 **tablespoon butter or margarine**
2 **tablespoons honey**
1 **cup toasted oat cereal, any flavor**
½ **cup coarsely broken pecans**
½ **cup thin pretzel sticks, broken in half**
½ **cup raisins**
1 **cup "M&M's"® Chocolate Mini Baking Bits**

In large heavy skillet over low heat, melt butter; add honey and stir until blended. Add cereal, nuts, pretzels and raisins, stirring until all pieces are evenly coated. Continue cooking over low heat about 10 minutes, stirring frequently. Remove from heat; immediately spread on waxed paper until cool. Add "M&M's"® Chocolate Mini Baking Bits. Store in tightly covered container.
Makes about 3½ cups

Maple-Cinnamon Almonds

Nicole's Cheddar Crisps

1¾ cups all-purpose flour
½ cup yellow cornmeal
¾ teaspoon sugar
¾ teaspoon salt
½ teaspoon baking soda
½ cup (1 stick) butter or margarine
1½ cups (6 ounces) shredded sharp Cheddar cheese
½ cup cold water
2 tablespoons white vinegar
Coarsely ground black pepper

Mix flour, cornmeal, sugar, salt and baking soda in large bowl. Cut in butter with pastry blender until mixture resembles coarse crumbs. Stir in cheese, water and vinegar with fork until mixture forms soft dough. Cover dough and refrigerate 1 hour or freeze 30 minutes until firm.

Preheat oven to 375°F. Grease 2 large cookie sheets. Divide dough into 4 pieces. Roll each piece into paper-thin circle (about 13 inches in diameter) on floured surface. Sprinkle with pepper; press pepper firmly into dough.

Cut each circle into 8 wedges; place wedges on prepared cookie sheets. Bake about 10 minutes or until crisp. Store in airtight container for up to 3 days.

Makes 32 crisps

Toffee Popcorn Crunch

10 cups popped popcorn
1 cup whole almonds
1¾ cups (10-ounce package) SKOR® English Toffee Bits
⅔ cup light corn syrup

1. Heat oven to 275°F. Grease large roasting pan (or two 13×9×2-inch baking pans).

2. Place popcorn and almonds in prepared pan. Combine toffee bits and corn syrup in heavy medium saucepan. Cook over medium heat, stirring constantly, until toffee is melted (about 12 minutes). Pour over popcorn mixture; stir until evenly coated.

3. Bake 30 minutes, stirring frequently. Remove from oven; stir every 2 minutes until slightly cooled. Cool completely. Store in tightly covered container in cool, dry place.

Makes about 1½ pounds popcorn

Note: For best results, do *not* double this recipe.

Soft Pretzels

1¼ cups milk
4 to 4½ cups all-purpose flour, divided
¼ cup sugar
1 package active dry yeast
1 teaspoon baking powder
1 teaspoon garlic salt
½ cup unsalted butter, melted
2 tablespoons baking soda
  Coarse salt, sesame seeds or poppy seeds

1. Heat milk in small saucepan over low heat until temperature reaches 120°F to 130°F.

2. Combine 3 cups flour, sugar, yeast, baking powder and garlic salt in large bowl. Add milk and butter. Beat vigorously 2 minutes. Add remaining flour, ¼ cup at a time, until dough begins to pull away from side of bowl.

3. Turn out dough onto lightly floured surface; flatten slightly. Knead 10 minutes or until smooth and elastic, adding flour if necessary to prevent sticking.

4. Shape dough into ball. Place in large, lightly oiled bowl; turn dough over once to oil surface. Cover with towel; let rise in warm place about 30 minutes.

5. Divide dough into 18 equal pieces. Roll each piece into 22-inch-long rope on lightly oiled surface. Form rope into "U" shape. About 2 inches from each end, cross dough. Cross second time. Fold loose ends up to rounded part of "U"; press ends to seal. Turn pretzels over so that ends are on underside and reshape if necessary. Cover with towel; let rest 20 minutes.

6. Preheat oven to 400°F. Grease baking sheets or line with parchment paper. Fill large Dutch oven ¾ full with water. Bring to a boil over high heat. Add baking soda. Carefully drop pretzels, 3 at a time, into boiling water for 10 seconds. Remove with slotted spoon. Place on prepared baking sheets. Sprinkle with coarse salt, sesame seeds or poppy seeds.

7. Bake 15 minutes or until golden brown. Place on wire rack.

Makes 18 large pretzels

Gingerbread Caramel Corn

**10 cups popped, lightly salted popcorn (about ⅔ cup unpopped *or* 1 package
    [3½ ounces] microwave popcorn)**
1 cup lightly salted roasted cashews (optional)
1 cup packed dark brown sugar
½ cup butter
¼ cup light corn syrup
1 teaspoon ground ginger
1 teaspoon ground cinnamon
½ teaspoon baking soda

1. Preheat oven to 250°F. Line 17×11-inch shallow roasting pan with foil or use disposable foil roasting pan.

2. Combine popcorn and cashews in prepared pan; set aside.

3. Combine sugar, butter and syrup in heavy 1½- or 2-quart saucepan. Bring to a boil over medium heat, stirring constantly. Wash down sugar crystals with pastry brush, if necessary.

4. Attach candy thermometer to side of pan, making sure bulb is submerged in sugar mixture but not touching bottom of pan. Continue boiling, without stirring, about 5 minutes or until sugar mixture reaches soft-crack stage (290°F) on candy thermometer. Remove from heat; stir in ginger, cinnamon and baking soda. Immediately drizzle sugar mixture slowly over popcorn mixture; stir until evenly coated.

5. Bake 1 hour, stirring quickly every 15 minutes. Transfer to large baking sheet lined with foil; spread caramel corn in single layer. Cool completely, about 10 minutes. Store in airtight container at room temperature.

Makes about 10 cups caramel corn

People Chow

1 cup butter or margarine
1 package (12 ounces) semisweet chocolate chips
18 cups dry cereal (mixture of bite-sized wheat, corn and rice cereal squares or toasted oat cereal)
2 cups nuts (cashews, peanuts, mixed nuts, pecans or walnuts)
6 cups powdered sugar

Melt butter and chocolate chips in medium-sized heavy saucepan over low heat; cook and stir until melted and smooth. Place cereal and nuts in very large bowl. Pour chocolate mixture over cereal and nuts; mix until thoroughly coated. Sprinkle with sugar, 2 cups at a time, carefully folding and mixing until thoroughly coated.

Makes about 24 cups

Gingerbread Caramel Corn

Fruited Granola

3 cups uncooked quick-cooking oats
1 cup sliced unblanched almonds
1 cup honey
3 tablespoons butter or margarine, melted
½ cup wheat germ or honey wheat germ
1 teaspoon ground cinnamon
3 cups whole grain or whole wheat cereal flakes
½ cup dried blueberries or golden raisins
½ cup dried cranberries or tart cherries
½ cup dried banana chips or chopped pitted dates

1. Preheat oven to 325°F. Spread oats and almonds in single layer in 13×9-inch baking pan. Bake 15 minutes or until lightly toasted, stirring frequently. Remove pan from oven; set aside.

2. Combine honey, butter, wheat germ and cinnamon in large bowl until well blended. Add oats and almonds; toss to coat completely. Spread mixture in single layer in baking pan.

3. Bake 20 minutes or until golden brown. Cool completely in pan on wire rack. Break mixture into chunks.

4. Combine oat chunks, cereal, blueberries, cranberries and banana chips in large bowl.

5. Store in airtight container at room temperature up to 2 weeks.

Makes about 10 cups

Peppered Pecans

3 tablespoons butter *or* margarine
3 cloves garlic, minced
1½ teaspoons TABASCO® brand Pepper Sauce
½ teaspoon salt
3 cups pecan halves

Preheat oven to 250°F. Melt butter in small skillet. Add garlic, TABASCO® Sauce and salt; cook 1 minute. Toss pecans with butter mixture; spread in single layer on baking sheet. Bake 1 hour or until pecans are crisp, stirring occasionally.

Makes 3 cups

Fruited Granola

Santa Fe Trail Mix

1½ cups pecan halves
1 cup cashews
¾ cup roasted shelled pistachio nuts
½ cup pine nuts
⅓ cup roasted sunflower seeds
3 tablespoons butter
2½ teaspoons ground cumin
¼ teaspoon garlic powder
¼ cup plus 1 tablespoon chili sauce
1 chipotle chili in adobo sauce, about 3 inches long
1 tablespoon frozen orange juice concentrate, thawed
Nonstick cooking spray
1 tablespoon dried cilantro leaves, divided

1. Preheat oven to 300°F. Line 14×11-inch baking sheet with foil.

2. Combine pecans, cashews, pistachios, pine nuts and sunflower seeds in large bowl.

3. Combine butter, cumin and garlic powder in small microwavable bowl. Microwave at HIGH 45 to 50 seconds or until butter is melted and foamy; stir to blend.

4. Place butter mixture, chili sauce, chipotle chili and orange juice concentrate in food processor or blender; process until smooth. Pour sauce over nut mixture; stir to coat evenly. Spread mixture in single layer on prepared baking sheet.

5. Bake about 1 hour, stirring every 10 minutes. Remove from oven and spray mixture evenly with cooking spray. Sprinkle 1½ teaspoons cilantro over mixture. Stir mixture and repeat with additional cooking spray and remaining cilantro. Set baking sheet on wire rack to cool. Leave uncovered at least 1 hour before storing in airtight container or resealable plastic food storage bag. *Makes 4 cups*

Peppy Snack Mix

3 plain rice cakes, broken into bite-size pieces
1½ cups bite-size frosted shredded wheat biscuit cereal
¾ cup pretzel sticks, halved
3 tablespoons reduced-fat margarine, melted
2 teaspoons low-sodium Worcestershire sauce
¾ teaspoon chili powder
⅛ to ¼ teaspoon ground red pepper

Preheat oven to 300°F. Combine rice cakes, cereal and pretzels in 13×9-inch baking pan. Combine margarine, Worcestershire, chili powder and pepper in small bowl. Drizzle over cereal mixture; toss to combine. Bake 20 minutes, stirring after 10 minutes. *Makes 6 (⅔-cup) servings*

Yuletide Twisters

1 (6-ounce) package premier white baking bars
4 teaspoons fat-free (skim) milk
4 teaspoons light corn syrup
8 ounces reduced-salt pretzel twists (about 80)
 Cookie decorations, colored sugar or chocolate sprinkles

1. Line baking sheet with waxed paper; set aside.

2. Melt baking bars in small saucepan over low heat, stirring constantly. Stir in skim milk and corn syrup. Do not remove saucepan from heat.

3. Holding pretzel with fork, dip 1 side of each pretzel into melted mixture to coat. Place, coated side up, on prepared baking sheet; immediately sprinkle with desired decorations. Refrigerate until firm, 15 to 20 minutes. *Makes 10 servings*

Chocolate Twisters: Substitute semisweet chocolate chips for premier white baking bars.

Caramel Dippity Do's: Heat 1 cup nonfat caramel sauce and ⅓ cup finely chopped pecans in small saucepan until warm. Pour into small serving bowl. Serve with pretzels for dipping. Makes 8 servings (about 2 tablespoons each).

Chocolate Dippity Do's: Heat 1 cup nonfat hot fudge sauce and ⅓ cup finely chopped pecans or walnuts in small saucepan until warm. Pour into small serving bowl. Serve with pretzels for dipping. Makes 8 servings (about 2 tablespoons each).

Sugared Nuts

 1 cup sugar
 ½ cup water
2½ cups unsalted mixed nuts
 1 teaspoon vanilla

Grease baking sheet; set aside.

Combine sugar and water in medium saucepan. Cook, stirring constantly, over medium heat until sugar dissolves. Add nuts and vanilla. Cook, stirring occasionally, until water evaporates and nuts are sugary, about 12 minutes.

Spread on prepared baking sheet, separating nuts. Let stand until cooled.

Makes about 1 pound

Sun-Dried Tomato Pizza Snack Mix

2 cups wheat cereal squares
2 cups unsweetened puffed corn cereal
2 cups crisp rice cereal
2 cups square mini cheese crackers
1 cup roasted sunflower seeds
3 tablespoons grated Parmesan cheese
3 tablespoons butter
2 tablespoons olive oil
2 teaspoons dried Italian seasoning
1½ teaspoons garlic powder
¼ cup tomato sauce
1 teaspoon balsamic vinegar
¼ teaspoon sugar
⅛ teaspoon salt
8 to 9 sun-dried tomatoes packed in oil, diced

1. Preheat oven to 250°F. Spray 13×9-inch baking pan with nonstick cooking spray.

2. Combine cereals, cheese crackers and sunflower seeds in large bowl; set aside.

3. Combine cheese, butter, oil, Italian seasoning and garlic powder in medium bowl. Microwave at HIGH 1 to 1½ minutes until foamy and herbs release their aromas. Stir in tomato sauce, vinegar, sugar and salt. Pour over cereal mixture; stir well to coat. Place in prepared pan and spread in single layer.

4. Bake 55 to 60 minutes, stirring every 15 minutes. Stir in sun-dried tomatoes 15 minutes before finished baking. Cool in pan on wire rack about 2 hours, leaving uncovered until mixture is crisp and tomato pieces have lost their moisture. Store in airtight container or resealable plastic food storage bag. *Makes 7 cups*

Deviled Mixed Nuts

3 tablespoons vegetable oil
2 cups assorted unsalted nuts, such as peanuts, almonds, Brazil nuts or walnuts
2 tablespoons sugar
1 teaspoon paprika
½ teaspoon chili powder
½ teaspoon curry powder
½ teaspoon ground cumin
½ teaspoon ground coriander
½ teaspoon black pepper
¼ teaspoon salt

Heat oil in large skillet over medium heat; cook and stir nuts in hot oil 2 to 3 minutes or until browned. Combine remaining ingredients in small bowl; sprinkle over nuts. Stir to coat evenly. Heat 1 to 2 minutes more. Drain nuts on wire rack lined with paper towels. Serve warm. *Makes 2 cups*

Sun-Dried Tomato Pizza Snack Mix

Crispy Ranch Breadsticks

2 tablespoons dry ranch party dip mix
2 tablespoons sour cream
1 package (10 ounces) refrigerated pizza dough
  Butter, melted

1. Preheat oven to 400°F. Grease baking sheets or line with parchment paper. Combine dip mix and sour cream in small bowl; set aside.

2. Unroll pizza dough on lightly floured work surface. Shape dough into 16×10-inch rectangle. Brush with melted butter. Spread dip mixture evenly over top of dough; cut into 24 (10-inch) strips. Form into desired shapes.

3. Place breadsticks ½ inch apart on prepared baking sheets. Bake 10 minutes or until golden brown. Serve immediately or place on wire rack to cool.

Makes 24 breadsticks

Crispy Spiced Nut Breadsticks: Place 1 cup finely chopped pecans and 1 tablespoon vegetable oil in plastic bag; toss to coat. Combine ¼ teaspoon chili powder, ¼ teaspoon ground cumin, ¼ teaspoon curry powder, ⅛ teaspoon ground cinnamon and dash of ground red pepper in small bowl. Add to nuts; toss to coat. Place nuts in small pan over medium heat and stir constantly until nuts are lightly toasted. Sprinkle nut mixture with 1 teaspoon garlic salt; cool to room temperature. Instead of spreading dough with sour cream mixture, sprinkle ½ cup spiced nuts over dough (store remaining nuts in tightly covered container). Cut into 24 (10-inch) strips. Form into desired shapes. Bake as directed.

Chocolate & Fruit Snack Mix

  ½ cup (1 stick) butter or margarine
  2 tablespoons sugar
  1 tablespoon HERSHEY₂S Cocoa or HERSHEY₂S Dutch Processed Cocoa
  ½ teaspoon ground cinnamon
  3 cups bite-size crisp rice squares cereal
  3 cups bite-size crisp wheat squares cereal
  2 cups toasted oat cereal rings
  1 cup cashews
1½ cups (6-ounce package) dried fruit bits
  1 cup HERSHEY₂S Semi-Sweet Chocolate Chips

1. Place butter in 4-quart microwave-safe bowl. Microwave at HIGH (100%) 1 minute or until melted; stir in sugar, cocoa and cinnamon. Add cereals and nuts; stir until evenly coated. Microwave at HIGH 3 minutes, stirring after each minute; stir in dried fruit. Microwave at HIGH 3 minutes, stirring after each minute.

2. Cool completely; stir in chocolate chips. Store in tightly covered container in cool, dry place.

Makes about 11 cups

Top to bottom: Crispy Spiced Nut Breadsticks and
Crispy Ranch Breadsticks

Antipasto Crescent Bites

2 ounces cream cheese (do not use reduced-fat or fat-free cream cheese)
1 package (8 ounces) refrigerated crescent roll dough
1 egg plus 1 tablespoon water, beaten
4 strips roasted red pepper, cut into 3×¾-inch-long strips
2 large marinated artichoke hearts, cut in half lengthwise to ¾-inch width
1 thin slice Genoa or other salami, cut into 4 strips
4 small stuffed green olives, cut into halves

1. Preheat oven to 375°F. Cut cream cheese into 16 equal pieces, about 1 teaspoon per piece; set aside.

2. Remove dough from package. Unroll on lightly floured surface. Cut each triangle of dough in half to form 2 triangles. Brush outer edges of triangle lightly with egg mixture.

3. Wrap 1 pepper strip around 1 piece of cream cheese. Place on dough triangle. Fold over and pinch edges to seal; repeat with remaining pepper strips. Place 1 piece artichoke heart and 1 piece of cream cheese on dough triangle. Fold over and pinch edges to seal; repeat with remaining pieces of artichoke hearts. Wrap 1 strip salami around 1 piece of cream cheese. Place on dough triangle. Fold over and pinch edges to seal; repeat with remaining salami. Place 2 olive halves and 1 piece of cream cheese on dough triangle. Fold over and pinch edges to seal; repeat with remaining olives. Place evenly spaced on ungreased baking sheet. Brush with egg mixture.

4. Bake 12 to 14 minutes or until golden brown. Cool on wire rack. Store in airtight container in refrigerator.

5. Reheat on baking sheet in preheated 325°F oven 7 to 8 minutes or until warmed through. Do not microwave. *Makes 16 pieces*

Citrus Candied Nuts

1 egg white
1½ cups whole almonds
1½ cups pecan halves
1 cup powdered sugar
2 tablespoons lemon juice
2 teaspoons grated orange peel
1 teaspoon grated lemon peel
⅛ teaspoon ground nutmeg

Preheat oven to 300°F. Generously grease 15½×10½×1-inch jelly-roll pan. Beat egg white in medium bowl with electric mixer on high speed until soft peaks form. Add almonds and pecans; stir until coated. Stir in powdered sugar, lemon juice, orange peel, lemon peel and nutmeg. Turn onto prepared pan, spreading nuts in single layer.

Bake 30 minutes, stirring after 20 minutes. Turn off oven. Let nuts stand in oven 15 minutes. Remove nuts from pan to sheet of foil. Cool completely. Store up to 2 weeks in airtight container. *Makes about 3 cups*

Antipasto Crescent Bites

Sweet and Spicy Snack Mix

6 cups popped corn
3 cups miniature pretzels
1½ cups pecan halves
⅔ cup packed brown sugar
⅓ cup butter or margarine
1 teaspoon ground cinnamon
¼ teaspoon ground red pepper

Microwave Directions

1. Combine popped corn, pretzels and nuts in large bowl.

2. Place brown sugar, butter, cinnamon and red pepper in 2-cup microwavable cup. Microwave at HIGH 1½ minutes or until bubbly.

3. Pour butter mixture over popcorn mixture; toss with rubber spatula until well mixed.

Makes about 10 cups

Cinnamon Popcorn

10 cups air-popped popcorn (½ cup unpopped)
1½ cups (7 ounces) coarsely chopped pecans
¾ cup granulated sugar
¾ cup packed light brown sugar
½ cup light corn syrup
3 tablespoons *Frank's® RedHot®* Cayenne Pepper Sauce
2 tablespoons honey
6 tablespoons (¾ stick) unsalted butter, at room temperature, cut into thin pats
1 tablespoon ground cinnamon

1. Preheat oven to 250°F. Place popcorn and pecans in 5-quart ovenproof bowl or Dutch oven. Bake 15 minutes.

2. Combine sugars, corn syrup, **Frank's RedHot** Sauce and honey in 2-quart saucepan. Bring to a full boil over medium-high heat, stirring just until sugars dissolve. Boil about 6 to 8 minutes or until soft crack stage (290°F on candy thermometer). *Do not stir.* Remove from heat.

3. Gradually add butter and cinnamon to sugar mixture, stirring gently until well blended. Pour over popcorn, tossing to coat evenly.* Spread popcorn mixture on greased baking sheets, using two forks. Cool completely. Break into bite-size pieces. Store in airtight container up to 2 weeks.

Makes 18 cups

*If popcorn mixture sets too quickly, return to oven to rewarm. Popcorn mixture may be shaped into 3-inch balls while warm, if desired.

Prep Time: 15 minutes
Cook Time: 8 to 10 minutes

Sweet and Spicy Snack Mix

Pizza Breadsticks

1 package (¼ ounce) active dry yeast
¾ cup warm water (105° to 115°F)
2½ cups all-purpose flour
½ cup (2 ounces) shredded part-skim mozzarella cheese
¼ cup (1 ounce) shredded Parmesan cheese
¼ cup chopped red bell pepper
1 green onion with top, sliced
1 medium clove garlic, minced
½ teaspoon dried basil leaves, crushed
½ teaspoon dried oregano leaves, crushed
¼ teaspoon red pepper flakes (optional)
¼ teaspoon salt
1 tablespoon olive oil

1. Preheat oven to 400°F. Spray 2 large nonstick baking sheets with nonstick cooking spray; set aside.

2. Sprinkle yeast over warm water in small bowl; stir until yeast dissolves. Let stand 5 minutes or until bubbly.

3. Meanwhile, place all remaining ingredients except olive oil in food processor; process a few seconds to combine. With food processor running, gradually add yeast mixture and olive oil. Process just until mixture forms a ball. (Add an additional 2 tablespoons flour if dough is too sticky.)

4. Transfer dough to lightly floured surface; knead 1 minute. Let dough rest 5 minutes. Roll out dough with lightly floured rolling pin to form 14×8-inch rectangle; cut dough crosswise into ½-inch-wide strips. Twist dough strips; place on prepared baking sheets.

5. Bake 14 to 16 minutes or until lightly browned.

Makes 14 servings

Harvest-Time Popcorn

2 tablespoons vegetable oil
1 cup popcorn kernels
2 cans (1¾ ounces each) shoestring potatoes (3 cups)
1 cup salted mixed nuts or peanuts
¼ cup margarine, melted
1 teaspoon dill weed
1 teaspoon Worcestershire sauce
½ teaspoon lemon-pepper seasoning
¼ teaspoon garlic powder
¼ teaspoon onion salt

1. Heat oil in 4-quart saucepan over high heat until hot. Add popcorn kernels. Cover pan; shake continuously over heat until popping stops. Popcorn should measure 2 quarts. Do not add butter or salt.

2. Preheat oven to 325°F. Combine popcorn, shoestring potatoes and nuts in large roasting pan. Set aside.

3. Combine margarine, dill, Worcestershire sauce, lemon-pepper seasoning, garlic powder and onion salt in small bowl.

4. Pour evenly over popcorn mixture, stirring until evenly coated.

5. Bake 8 to 10 minutes, stirring once. Let stand at room temperature until cool. Store in airtight containers.

Makes 2½ quarts

Cheesy Sun Crisps

2 cups (8 ounces) shredded Cheddar cheese
½ cup grated Parmesan cheese
½ cup sunflower oil margarine, softened
3 tablespoons water
1 cup all-purpose flour
¼ teaspoon salt (optional)
1 cup uncooked quick oats
⅔ cup roasted, salted sunflower seeds

Beat cheeses, margarine and water in bowl until blended. Mix in flour and salt. Stir in oats and sunflower seeds until combined. Shape into 12-inch-long roll; wrap securely. Refrigerate about 4 hours or up to 1 week.

Preheat oven to 400°F. Lightly grease cookie sheets. Cut roll into ⅛- to ¼-inch slices; flatten each slice slightly. Place on prepared cookie sheets. Bake 8 to 10 minutes or until edges are light golden brown. Remove immediately; cool on wire rack.

Makes 4 to 5 dozen crackers

*Favorite recipe from **National Sunflower Association***

Harvest-Time Popcorn

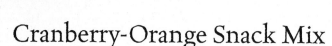

Cranberry-Orange Snack Mix

2 cups oatmeal cereal squares
2 cups corn cereal squares
2 cups mini pretzels
1 cup whole almonds
¼ cup butter
⅓ cup frozen orange juice concentrate, thawed
3 tablespoons packed brown sugar
1 teaspoon ground cinnamon
¾ teaspoon ground ginger
¼ teaspoon ground nutmeg
⅔ cup dried cranberries

1. Preheat oven to 250°F. Spray 13×9-inch baking pan with nonstick cooking spray.

2. Combine cereal squares, pretzels and almonds in large bowl; set aside.

3. Melt butter in medium microwavable bowl at HIGH 45 to 60 seconds. Stir in orange juice concentrate, brown sugar, cinnamon, ginger and nutmeg until blended. Pour over cereal mixture; stir well to coat. Place in prepared pan and spread in single layer.

4. Bake 50 minutes, stirring every 10 minutes. Stir in cranberries. Let cool in pan on wire rack, leaving uncovered until mixture is crisp. Store in airtight container or resealable plastic food storage bags. *Makes 8 cups snack mix*

Barbecued Peanuts

¼ cup barbecue sauce
2 tablespoons butter or margarine, melted
¾ teaspoon garlic salt
⅛ teaspoon ground red pepper*
1 jar (16 ounces) dry roasted lightly salted peanuts

*For Spicy Barbecued Peanuts, increase ground red pepper to ¼ teaspoon.

1. Preheat oven to 325°F. Grease 13×9-inch baking pan. Set aside.

2. Whisk barbecue sauce, melted butter, garlic salt and pepper in medium bowl with wire whisk until well blended. Add peanuts; toss until evenly coated with wooden spoon.

3. Spread peanuts in single layer in prepared baking pan.

4. Bake 20 to 22 minutes or until peanuts are glazed, stirring occasionally. Cool completely in pan on wire rack, stirring occasionally to prevent peanuts from sticking together.

5. Spoon into clean, dry decorative tin; cover. Store tightly covered at room temperature up to 2 weeks. *Makes about 4 cups*

Cranberry-Orange Snack Mix

GLORIOUS GIFTS IN A JAR

Cranberry Pecan Muffin Mix

1¾ cups all-purpose flour
1 cup dried cranberries
¾ cup chopped pecans
½ cup packed light brown sugar
2½ teaspoons baking powder
½ teaspoon salt

1. Layer ingredients attractively in any order in 1-quart food storage jar with tight-fitting lid. Pack ingredients down slightly before adding another layer.

2. Cover top of jar with fabric; attach recipe (below) with raffia or ribbon.

Makes 1 (1-quart) jar

Cranberry Pecan Muffins

1 jar Cranberry Pecan Muffin Mix
¾ cup milk
¼ cup (½ stick) butter, melted
1 egg, beaten

1. Preheat oven to 400°F. Grease or paper-line 12 regular-size (2½-inch) muffin cups.

2. Pour contents of jar into large bowl. Combine milk, butter and egg in small bowl until blended; stir into jar mixture just until moistened. Spoon evenly into prepared muffin cups.

3. Bake 16 to 18 minutes or until toothpick inserted in centers comes out clean. Cool in pan on wire rack 5 minutes; remove from pan and cool completely on wire rack.

Makes 12 muffins

Honey Strawberry Preserves

6 cups sliced strawberries
2 boxes (1¾ ounces each) powdered pectin
1¾ cups honey
2 tablespoons lemon juice

Combine strawberries and pectin in large saucepan; crush berries to blend completely. Bring mixture to a full rolling boil over medium-high heat. Boil hard 1 minute, stirring constantly. Stir in honey and lemon juice; return to a full rolling boil. Boil hard 5 minutes, stirring constantly. Remove from heat. Skim off foam. Ladle into clean, hot canning jars to within ¼ inch of tops. Seal according to manufacturer's directions. Place jars on rack in canner. Process 10 minutes in boiling water bath with boiling water 2 inches above jar tops. Remove jars from canner. Place on thick cloth or wire rack; cool away from drafts. After 12 hours test lids for proper seal; remove rings from sealed jars. *Makes 3 pints*

*Favorite recipe from **National Honey Board***

Honey Citrus Syrup

½ cup honey
¼ cup lemon juice
¼ cup orange juice

Combine all ingredients in small bowl; stir until well blended. Refrigerate in airtight container until ready to use. Use syrup to sweeten tea and glaze fruits.

Makes 1 cup

*Favorite recipe from **National Honey Board***

Honey Chocolate Sauce

1½ cups honey
1½ cups unsweetened cocoa
2 tablespoons butter or margarine

Combine all ingredients; mix well. Cover with waxed paper and microwave at HIGH (100% power) 2 to 2½ minutes, stirring after 1 minute. Pour into sterilized gift jars. Keep refrigerated. *Makes 2½ cups*

*Favorite recipe from **National Honey Board***

Clockwise from left: Honey Strawberry Preserves,
Honey Citrus Syrup and Honey Chocolate Sauce

Italian Salad Dressing

½ cup extra-virgin olive oil
¼ cup Basil-Garlic Champagne Vinegar (recipe follows)
1 teaspoon Dijon mustard
½ teaspoon salt
½ teaspoon sugar
¼ teaspoon black pepper

1. Whisk oil, Basil-Garlic Champagne Vinegar, mustard, salt, sugar and pepper in small bowl with wire whisk until well blended.

2. Place neck of funnel in clean, dry decorative bottle. Line funnel with double layer of cheesecloth or coffee filter.

3. Pour mixture into funnel; discard solids. Seal bottle. Store in refrigerator up to 1 month.

Makes about ¾ cup

Basil-Garlic Champagne Vinegar

¼ cup basil leaves
4 cloves garlic
4 dried hot red peppers
1¼ cups champagne or white wine vinegar

1. Separate basil leaves. Wash in cold water. Repeat several times to remove sand and grit. Pat dry with paper towels.

2. Place basil leaves, garlic and peppers in jar.

3. Pour vinegar into small nonaluminum saucepan. Heat until very hot. Do not boil. (If vinegar boils, it will become cloudy.) Remove saucepan from heat. Pour vinegar into jar; cover.

4. Shake jar several times to distribute basil leaves. Refrigerate at least 7 days, shaking occasionally.

5. To transfer vinegar to clean, dry decorative glass bottle with tight-fitting lid, line a funnel with double layer of cheesecloth or coffee filter.

6. Place neck of funnel into bottle. Pour vinegar mixture into funnel. Cover and store in cool, dark place up to 2 months.

Makes 2 cups

Left to right: Italian Salad Dressing and Basil-Garlic
Champagne Vinegar

Roasted Pepper & Tomato Salsa

3 yellow or red bell peppers
2 poblano peppers
1 large onion
2 tablespoons olive oil
4 cloves garlic, minced
1 teaspoon dried oregano leaves
¾ teaspoon salt
½ teaspoon black pepper
2 cans (14½ ounces each) diced tomatoes
¾ cup tomato juice
¼ cup chopped fresh cilantro
1 tablespoon lime juice

1. Preheat oven to 350°F. Chop peppers and onion into ¾-inch pieces. Combine peppers, onion, olive oil, garlic, oregano, salt and black pepper in large bowl; toss to coat. Spread onto two 15×10×1-inch baking pans. Bake 20 minutes or until peppers and onion are lightly browned, stirring after 10 minutes.

2. Combine roasted vegetables and remaining ingredients in large bowl. Spoon into 4 labeled 1½-cup storage containers. Store in refrigerator up to 10 days or freeze up to 2 months.   *Makes 4 (1½-cup) containers*

Crock of Spice for Apple Cider

12 cinnamon sticks, broken into small pieces
¼ cup whole cloves
¼ cup allspice berries
¼ cup juniper berries
1 tablespoon dried orange peel, chopped
1 tablespoon dried lemon peel, chopped
1 teaspoon ground nutmeg

Combine all ingredients in small bowl until well blended. Spoon into airtight container or decorative glass jar with tight-fitting lid; cover. To prepare spiced cider, measure 1 heaping teaspoon spice mixture for each mug of cider into large saucepan. Simmer cider with spices for 5 minutes. Strain before serving.

Gift Tip: Put mixture in crock or attractive container and give with jug of country apple cider from your favorite farm stand or market. Include above instructions for making spiced cider on a recipe card with the gift.

Variation: Pack into small bags you have made from Christmas fabrics or into muslin bouquet garni bags available at kitchen or specialty stores. Use like tea bags to flavor mugs of hot cider or mulled wine.

Roasted Pepper & Tomato Salsa

Chocolate-Cherry Chutney

2 jars (16 ounces each) maraschino cherries
8 ounces semisweet chocolate, coarsely chopped
1 can (5 ounces) evaporated milk
1 cup powdered sugar
1½ cups slivered or chopped toasted almonds
1 cup white chocolate chips

1. Drain cherries, reserving ¼ cup juice. Coarsely chop cherries; set aside.

2. Combine chocolate and evaporated milk in large microwavable bowl. Heat at HIGH 3 to 4 minutes or until melted, stirring after 2 minutes. Add powdered sugar and reserved cherry juice. Microwave 1 minute; stir until smooth. Stir in chopped cherries, toasted almonds and white chocolate chips.

3. Spoon into 4 labeled 1¼-cup containers. Store refrigerated up to 4 weeks.

Makes 4 (1¼-cup) containers

Tip: This chunky, chocolatey treat is fabulous served over pound cake, ice cream or other desserts.

Spicy German Mustard

½ cup mustard seeds
2 tablespoons dry mustard
½ cup cold water
1 cup cider vinegar
1 small onion, chopped (about ¼ cup)
3 tablespoons packed brown sugar
2 cloves garlic, minced
¾ teaspoon salt
¼ teaspoon dried tarragon leaves
¼ teaspoon ground cinnamon

Combine mustard seeds, dry mustard and water in small bowl. Cover; let stand at least 4 hours or overnight.

Combine vinegar, onion, brown sugar, garlic, salt, tarragon and cinnamon in heavy stainless steel 1-quart saucepan. Bring to a boil over high heat; reduce heat to medium. Boil, uncovered, about 7 to 10 minutes until mixture is reduced by half.

Pour vinegar mixture through fine sieve into food processor bowl. Rinse saucepan; set aside. Add mustard mixture to vinegar mixture; process about 1 minute or until mustard seeds are chopped but not puréed. Pour into same saucepan. Cook over low heat until mustard is thick, stirring constantly. Store in airtight container or decorative gift jars up to 1 year in refrigerator.

Makes about 1 cup

Chocolate-Cherry Chutney

Sun-Dried Tomato Pesto

1 tablespoon vegetable oil
½ cup pine nuts
2 cloves garlic
1 jar (8 ounces) sun-dried tomatoes packed in oil, undrained
1 cup Italian parsley
½ cup grated Parmesan cheese
¼ cup coarsely chopped pitted calamata olives
2 teaspoons dried basil leaves
¼ teaspoon red pepper flakes

1. To toast pine nuts, heat oil in small skillet over medium-low heat. Add pine nuts; cook 30 to 45 seconds or until lightly browned, shaking pan constantly. Remove nuts from skillet with slotted spoon; drain on paper towels.

2. Combine pine nuts and garlic in food processor. Process using on/off pulses until finely chopped. Add undrained tomatoes; process until finely chopped. Add parsley, cheese, olives, basil and pepper; process until mixture resembles thick paste.

3. Spoon pesto into decorative crock or jar with tight-fitting lid; cover. Store in airtight container in refrigerator up to 1 month. *Makes about 1½ cups*

Mocha Espresso

2 tablespoons Mocha Espresso Mix (recipe follows)
6 ounces boiling water
Whipping cream, whipped (optional)

Spoon 2 tablespoons espresso mix into cup or mug. Add 6 ounces boiling water; stir. Serve with whipping cream, if desired. *Makes 1 serving*

Mocha Espresso Mix

4 ounces semisweet chocolate (squares or bars)
¾ cup nonfat dry milk powder
½ cup espresso powder
½ teaspoon ground cinnamon

1. Place chocolate on cutting board; shave into small pieces with paring knife.

2. Combine chocolate, dry milk powder, espresso powder and cinnamon in small bowl until well blended.

3. Spoon mixture into clean, dry decorative glass jar with tight-fitting lid; cover.

4. Store in airtight container at room temperature up to 1 month.

Makes about 1⅔ cups

Asian Spicy Sweet Mustard

1 jar (16 ounces) spicy brown mustard
1 cup peanut butter
¾ cup hoisin sauce
½ cup packed brown sugar

1. Combine mustard, peanut butter, hoisin sauce and brown sugar in medium bowl. Blend with wire whisk.

2. Spoon into 4 labeled 1-cup containers. Store refrigerated up to 4 weeks.

Makes 4 (1-cup) containers

Cracked Peppercorn Honey Mustard

2½ cups Dijon mustard
1 jar (9½ ounces) extra-grainy Dijon mustard
¾ cup honey
2 tablespoons cracked black pepper
1 tablespoon dried tarragon leaves (optional)

1. Combine Dijon mustard, grainy Dijon mustard, honey, pepper and tarragon in medium bowl. Blend with wire whisk.

2. Spoon into 4 labeled 1¼-cup containers. Store refrigerated up to 4 weeks.

Makes 4 (1¼-cup) containers

Spiced Fruit Butter

3 pounds apples, pears or peaches
¾ cup apple juice, pear nectar or peach nectar
1 to 2 teaspoons ground cinnamon
½ teaspoon ground nutmeg
⅛ teaspoon ground cloves
5 teaspoons EQUAL® FOR RECIPES *or* 16 packets EQUAL® sweetener
 ** *or* ⅔ cup EQUAL® SPOONFUL™**

• Peel and core or pit fruit; slice. Combine prepared fruit, fruit juice and spices in Dutch oven. Bring to boiling; cover and simmer 15 minutes or until fruit is very tender. Cool slightly.

• Purée in batches in blender or food processor or with food mill. Return to Dutch oven. Simmer, uncovered, over low heat until desired consistency, stirring frequently. (This will take 10 minutes to 1½ hours.)

• Remove from heat; stir in Equal®. Transfer to freezer containers or jars, leaving ½-inch headspace. Store up to 2 weeks in refrigerator or up to 3 months in freezer.

Makes about 3 cups

Top to bottom: Asian Spicy Sweet Mustard and
Cracked Peppercorn Honey Mustard

Easy Cocoa Mix

2 cups nonfat dry milk powder
1 cup sugar
¾ cup powdered non-dairy creamer
½ cup unsweetened cocoa powder
¼ teaspoon salt

Combine all ingredients in bowl until well blended. Spoon into 1-quart airtight container or decorative gift jar; cover. *Makes about 4 cups mix or 16 servings*

For single serving: Place rounded ¼ cup Easy Cocoa Mix in mug or cup; add ¾ cup boiling water. Stir until mix is dissolved. Top with sweetened whipped cream and marshmallows, if desired. Serve immediately.

Cocoa Mashmallow Mix: Prepare Easy Cocoa Mix in 2-quart airtight container as directed, adding 1 package (10½ ounces) miniature marshmallows.

For single serving: Place rounded ½ cup Cocoa Marshmallow Mix in mug or cup; add ¾ cup boiling water. Stir until mix is dissolved. Serve immediately.

Mocha Coffee Mix

1 cup nonfat dry milk powder
¾ cup granulated sugar
⅔ cup powdered non-dairy creamer
½ cup unsweetened cocoa powder
⅓ cup instant coffee, pressed through fine sieve
¼ cup packed brown sugar
1 teaspoon ground cinnamon
¼ teaspoon salt
¼ teaspoon ground nutmeg

Combine all ingredients in bowl until well blended. Spoon into 1-quart airtight container or decorative gift jar; cover.

Makes about 3½ cups mix or 10 to 12 servings

For single serving: Place rounded ¼ cup Mocha Coffee Mix in mug or cup; add ¾ cup boiling water. Stir until mix is dissolved. Serve immediately.

Unsweetened cocoa powder (without any additional ingredients) can be stored in an airtight container in a cool, dark place for up to two years.

Left to right: Easy Cocoa Mix and Mocha Coffee Mix

Carrot-Walnut Chutney

1 pound fresh carrots, peeled and chopped into ½-inch pieces
2 tablespoons vegetable oil
1½ cups chopped onions
¾ cup packed brown sugar
¼ cup apple cider vinegar
1 teaspoon ground allspice
1 teaspoon ground cumin
½ teaspoon ground cinnamon
½ teaspoon black pepper
¼ teaspoon salt
1 cup raisins
1½ cups chopped toasted walnuts

1. Place carrots and ⅓ cup water in large saucepan; cover. Bring to a boil over high heat; reduce heat to low. Simmer 8 to 10 minutes or until tender; drain.

2. Heat oil in large skillet over medium-high heat 1 minute. Add onions; cook and stir 6 to 8 minutes or until golden brown. Stir in brown sugar, vinegar, allspice, cumin, cinnamon, pepper and salt; simmer 1 minute. Add raisins; simmer 3 minutes. Remove from heat; stir in carrots and walnuts. Spoon into 4 labeled 1-cup containers. Store refrigerated up to 4 weeks. *Makes 4 (1-cup) containers*

Chunky Fruit Chutney

2 cans (15¼ ounces each) tropical fruit salad packed in light syrup and passion fruit juice
1 can (15 ounces) apricot halves in extra light syrup
1 cup chopped green bell pepper
1 cup chopped red bell pepper
¼ cup packed brown sugar
1 teaspoon curry powder
1 teaspoon onion powder
½ teaspoon salt
½ teaspoon garlic powder
½ teaspoon ground ginger
½ teaspoon red pepper flakes
½ teaspoon black pepper

1. Drain tropical fruit salad, reserving ½ cup juice. Drain apricots; discard syrup. Chop fruit salad and apricots into ½-inch pieces; set aside.

2. Combine bell peppers, reserved ½ cup juice and remaining ingredients in large skillet. Bring to a boil over high heat. Reduce heat to medium-high; simmer 6 to 8 minutes or until most liquid is evaporated and bell peppers are tender. Remove from heat. Stir in chopped fruit. Spoon into 4 labeled 1¼-cup containers. Store refrigerated up to 4 weeks. *Makes 4 (1¼-cup) containers*

Top to bottom: Carrot-Walnut Chutney and
Chunky Fruit Chutney

53

Spiced Peach Sauce

2 pounds frozen sliced unsweetened peaches, thawed
2 cups sugar
1½ teaspoons lemon juice
1½ teaspoons ground cinnamon
¼ teaspoon ground nutmeg

1. Combine peaches and thawing liquid, sugar, lemon juice, cinnamon and nutmeg in heavy, medium saucepan.

2. Bring to a boil over high heat. Boil 45 to 50 minutes or until thickened, stirring occasionally and breaking peaches into small pieces with back of wooden spoon. Remove saucepan from heat; cool completely.

3. Store in airtight container in refrigerator up to 2 months. *Makes about 3 cups*

Freezer Plum Conserve

4 (½-pint) jelly jars with lids
2 cans (16 ounces each) whole purple plums, drained and pitted
1 tablespoon grated orange peel
1 large orange, peeled and sectioned
4 cups sugar
1 cup raisins
½ cup chopped walnuts
¾ cup water
1 box (1¾ ounces) powdered fruit pectin

Rinse clean jars and lids with boiling water. Place plums, orange peel and orange sections in food processor or blender. Process until plums are chopped.

Stir sugar into plum mixture. Stir until well blended. Stir in raisins and walnuts. Let stand for 10 minutes, stirring occasionally.

Mix water and pectin in 1-quart saucepan. (Mixture may be lumpy.) Bring to a boil over high heat, stirring constantly. Boil and stir 1 minute. Stir hot pectin mixture into fruit mixture. Stir constantly for 3 minutes.

Ladle hot mixture into jars leaving ½-inch space at top. Run metal spatula around inside of jar to remove air bubbles. Wipe tops and sides of jar rims clean; quickly cover with lids. Let stand at room temperature up to 24 hours or until set. Store in freezer up to 12 months. Thaw jars in refrigerator overnight before using. Refrigerate after opening up to 6 months. *Makes about four ½-pint jars*

Herbed Vinegar

1½ cups white wine vinegar
½ cup fresh basil leaves

Pour vinegar into nonaluminum 2-quart saucepan. Heat until very hot, stirring occasionally. Do not boil. (If vinegar boils, it will become cloudy.)

Pour into glass bowl; add basil. Cover with plastic wrap. Refrigerate about 1 week until desired amount of flavor develops. Strain before using. Store in jar or bottle with tight-fitting lid in refrigerator for up to 6 months.

Makes about 1½ cups vinegar

Variation: Substitute 1 tablespoon of either fresh oregano, thyme, chervil or tarragon for the basil. Or, substitute cider vinegar for the wine vinegar.

Tip: It's important that glass bowl, storage jars and bottles are washed with hot soapy water, then rinsed well with very hot water before use.

Raspberry Vinegar

1½ cups white wine vinegar
½ cup sugar
1 cup fresh raspberries or sliced strawberries, crushed

Combine vinegar and sugar in nonaluminum 2-quart saucepan. Heat until very hot, stirring occasionally. Do not boil. (If vinegar boils, it will become cloudy.)

Pour into glass bowl; stir in raspberries. Cover with plastic wrap. Refrigerate about 1 week until desired amount of flavor develops. Strain through fine mesh sieve or cheesecloth twice. Store in jar or bottle with tight-fitting lid in refrigerator for up to 6 months.

Makes about 2 cups vinegar

Rich Chocolate Sauce

1 cup whipping cream
⅓ cup light corn syrup
1 cup (6 ounces) semisweet chocolate chips
1 to 2 tablespoons dark rum (optional)
1 teaspoon vanilla

Place cream and corn syrup in heavy 2-quart saucepan. Stir over medium heat until mixture boils. Remove from heat. Stir in chocolate, rum, if desired, and vanilla until chocolate is melted. Cool 10 minutes. Serve warm or pour into clean glass jars and seal tightly. Store up to 6 months in refrigerator. Reheat sauce over low heat before serving.

Makes about 1¾ cups sauce

Left to right: Herbed Vinegar and Raspberry Vinegar

Eggplant Chutney

2 large eggplant (2½ pounds), unpeeled, cut into ½-inch cubes
1 small onion, finely chopped
3 tablespoons minced garlic
3 tablespoons minced fresh ginger
3 tablespoons packed light brown sugar
1 teaspoon dried rosemary
1 teaspoon dried anise or fennel seeds
½ teaspoon dried thyme leaves
2 tablespoons balsamic vinegar
1 tablespoon dark sesame oil
¼ cup dark raisins
½ cup ⅓-less-salt chicken broth
2 tablespoons coarsely chopped walnuts

1. Preheat oven to 450°F. Arrange eggplant on 15×10-inch jelly-roll pan lined with foil. Add onion, garlic, ginger, brown sugar, rosemary, anise and thyme; toss to combine. Drizzle with vinegar and oil; stir to coat. Bake 1½ hours or until eggplant is browned and shriveled, stirring every 30 minutes.

2. Stir raisins into eggplant mixture and drizzle with chicken broth; bake 10 minutes or until broth is absorbed. Remove from oven; stir in walnuts. Cool. Serve on crackers or lavash as an appetizer or serve warm or at room temperature as a condiment or relish with roasted meats and poultry, if desired. Garnish with kale and orange slices, if desired. Store chutney in airtight container for up to 10 days in the refrigerator or 3 months in the freezer. *Makes about 2¾ cups*

Peach Preserves

2½ to 3 pounds ripe peaches (10 to 12 peaches)
2 tablespoons lemon juice
1 package (1¾ ounces) no-sugar-needed pectin
7¼ teaspoons EQUAL® FOR RECIPES *or* 24 packets EQUAL® sweetener
or 1 cup EQUAL® SPOONFUL™

• Peel, pit and finely chop peaches; measure 4 cups into saucepan. Stir in lemon juice and pectin. Let stand 10 minutes, stirring frequently. Cook and stir until boiling. Cook and stir 1 minute more. Remove from heat; stir in Equal®. Skim off foam.

• Immediately ladle into freezer containers or jars, leaving ½-inch headspace. Seal and label containers. Let stand at room temperature several hours or until set. Store up to 2 weeks in refrigerator or 6 months in freezer. *Makes 8 (½-pint) jars*

Zucchini Chow Chow

2 cups thinly sliced zucchini
2 cups thinly sliced yellow summer squash*
½ cup thinly sliced red onion
    Salt
1½ cups cider vinegar
1 to 1¼ cups sugar
1½ tablespoons pickling spice
1 cup thinly sliced carrots
1 small red bell pepper, thinly sliced

If yellow summer squash is not available, increase zucchini to 4 cups.

1. Sprinkle zucchini, summer squash and onion lightly with salt; let stand in colander 30 minutes. Rinse well with cold water; drain thoroughly. Pat dry with paper towels.

2. Combine vinegar, sugar and pickling spice in medium saucepan. Bring to a boil over high heat. Add carrots and bell pepper; bring to a boil. Remove from heat; cool to room temperature.

3. Spoon zucchini, summer squash, onion and carrot mixture into sterilized jars; cover and refrigerate up to 3 weeks. *Makes about 8 cups*

Champagne-Strawberry Freezer Jam

4 cups fresh strawberries (about 2 pints)
1½ cups champagne
3 cups sugar
1 box (1.75 ounces) fruit pectin for lower sugar recipes

1. Place strawberries in food processor or blender; process until pieces are about ¼ inch in size. Measure 3¼ cups; set aside.

2. Bring champagne to a boil over high heat in medium saucepan. Reduce heat to medium-low; simmer 10 minutes. Remove from heat; let stand 15 minutes. Return champagne to measuring cup; add enough water to equal 1 cup.

3. Combine sugar and pectin in medium bowl; blend well. Combine sugar mixture and champagne in large saucepan. Bring to a boil over medium-high heat, stirring constantly. Continue boiling 1 minute longer, stirring constantly. Remove from heat. Add strawberries; stir 1 minute.

4. Spoon into 5 labeled 1-cup freezer containers, leaving ½-inch space at top of each container. Cover with tight-fitting lids. Let stand at room temperature 24 hours to set. Refrigerate up to 3 weeks or freeze up to 6 months.

Makes 5 (1-cup) containers

Citrus-Plum Barbecue Sauce

2 containers (12 ounces each) orange juice concentrate
2 jars (12 ounces each) plum preserves
½ cup honey
½ cup tomato paste
¼ cup dry sherry
2 tablespoons minced ginger
2 tablespoons soy sauce
2 cloves garlic, minced
½ teaspoon salt
½ teaspoon black pepper

1. Combine all ingredients in large saucepan. Heat over medium-high heat until mixture begins to simmer. Reduce heat to medium-low; simmer 10 minutes. Cover and remove from heat. Cool 30 minutes.

2. Spoon into 4 labeled 12-ounce containers. Store refrigerated up to 3 weeks.

Makes 5½ to 6 cups

Oatmeal-Chip Cookie Mix in a Jar

⅔ cup all-purpose flour
½ teaspoon baking soda
½ teaspoon ground cinnamon
¼ teaspoon salt
⅓ cup packed brown sugar
⅓ cup granulated sugar
¾ cup NESTLÉ® TOLL HOUSE® Semi-Sweet Chocolate or Butterscotch Flavored Morsels
1½ cups quick or old-fashioned oats
½ cup chopped nuts

COMBINE flour, baking soda, cinnamon and salt in small bowl. Place flour mixture in 1-quart jar. Layer remaining ingredients in order listed above, pressing firmly after each layer. Seal with lid and decorate with fabric and ribbon.

Recipe to Attach
BEAT ½ cup (1 stick) softened butter or margarine, 1 large egg and ½ teaspoon vanilla extract in large mixer bowl until blended. Add cookie mix; mix well, breaking up any clumps. Drop by rounded tablespoon onto ungreased baking sheets. Bake in preheated 375°F. oven for 8 to 10 minutes. Cool on baking sheets for 2 minutes; remove to wire racks. Makes about 2 dozen cookies.

Citrus-Plum Barbecue Sauce

Rio Grande Salsa

- 1 tablespoon vegetable oil
- 1 onion, chopped
- 3 cloves garlic, minced
- 2 teaspoons ground cumin
- 1½ teaspoons chili powder
- 2 cans (14½ ounces each) diced tomatoes, drained
- 1 canned chipotle chili pepper, seeded and finely diced
- 1 teaspoon adobo sauce from canned chili pepper
- ½ cup chopped fresh cilantro
- ¾ teaspoon sugar
- ½ teaspoon salt

1. Heat oil in medium saucepan over medium-high heat until hot. Add onion and garlic. Cook and stir 5 minutes or until onion is tender. Add cumin and chili powder; cook 30 seconds, stirring frequently. Add tomatoes, chili pepper and adobo sauce. Reduce heat to medium-low. Simmer 10 to 12 minutes or until salsa is thickened, stirring occasionally.

2. Remove saucepan from heat; stir in cilantro, sugar and salt. Cool completely. Store in airtight container in refrigerator up to 3 weeks. *Makes about 3 cups*

Note: This salsa is very spicy. For a milder version, use only 1 teaspoon finely diced chipotle chili pepper.

Hot & Spicy Mustard

- ¼ cup whole yellow mustard seeds
- ¼ cup honey
- 3 tablespoons cider vinegar
- 2 tablespoons ground mustard
- 1 teaspoon salt
- ⅛ teaspoon ground cloves

1. Place ¼ cup water in small saucepan. Bring to a boil over high heat. Add mustard seeds. Cover saucepan; remove from heat. Let stand 1 hour or until liquid is absorbed.

2. Spoon mustard seeds into work bowl of food processor. Add honey, vinegar, ground mustard, salt and cloves to work bowl; process using on/off pulses until mixture is thickened and seeds are coarsely chopped, scraping down side of work bowl once with spatula. Refrigerate at least 1 day before serving.

3. Store in airtight container in refrigerator up to 3 weeks. *Makes about 1 cup*

Rio Grande Salsa

Homestyle Mixed Berry Freezer Jam

1 package (16 ounces) frozen mixed berries, thawed
3¾ cups sugar
2 teaspoons grated orange peel (optional)
1 pouch (3 ounces) liquid pectin
2 tablespoons orange juice

1. Place berries in food processor or blender; process until pieces are about ¼ inch in size. Combine berries, sugar and orange peel in large bowl; stir 2 minutes. Let stand 10 minutes.

2. Combine pectin and orange juice in small bowl; stir into berry mixture. Stir 2 minutes to blend thoroughly. Spoon into 4 labeled 1-cup freezer containers, leaving ½-inch space at top of each container. Cover with tight-fitting lids. Let stand 24 hours to set. Refrigerate up to 3 weeks or freeze up to 6 months.

Makes 4 (1-cup) containers

Cranberry-Peach Freezer Jam

3 cups (12 ounces) fresh or frozen cranberries, thawed
2 cups coarsely chopped fresh peaches
6 cups sugar
¾ cup peach nectar
1 teaspoon grated fresh ginger (optional)
2 pouches (3 ounces each) liquid pectin
¼ cup lemon juice

1. Place cranberries in food processor or blender; process until pieces are ⅛ inch in size. Transfer to large bowl. Place peaches in food processor or blender; process until pieces are ¼ inch in size. Add peaches, sugar, peach nectar and ginger to cranberries; stir 2 minutes. Let stand 10 minutes.

2. Combine pectin and lemon juice in small bowl; stir into fruit mixture. Stir 2 minutes to mix thoroughly.

3. Spoon into 7 labeled 1-cup freezer containers, leaving ½-inch space at top. Cover with tight-fitting lids. Let stand 24 hours to set. Refrigerate up to 3 weeks or freeze up to 6 months.

Makes 7 (1-cup) containers

Left to right: Homestyle Mixed Berry Freezer Jam and
Cranberry-Peach Freezer Jam

Texas Hot & Tangy BBQ Sauce

¼ cup vegetable oil
2 cups finely chopped onion
6 cloves garlic, minced
2 cups water
1 can (12 ounces) tomato paste
1 cup packed brown sugar
¾ cup apple cider vinegar
½ cup molasses
¼ cup Worcestershire sauce
2 tablespoons jalapeño pepper sauce
2 teaspoons chili powder
2 teaspoons ground cumin
½ teaspoon ground red pepper

1. Heat oil in large skillet over medium-high heat 1 minute. Add onions; cook and stir 8 to 10 minutes or until onions begin to brown. Add garlic; cook 2 minutes or until onions are golden. Add remaining ingredients. Stir with wire whisk until well blended. Reduce heat to medium-low; simmer 15 minutes, stirring occasionally. Cover and remove from heat. Cool 30 minutes.

2. Spoon into 4 labeled 12-ounce containers. Store refrigerated up to 3 weeks.

Makes 5 to 5½ cups

Hint: Take the chill out of winter with a summer-theme gift basket. Pack a picnic basket with a tablecloth, a festive jar filled with Texas Hot & Tangy BBQ Sauce, a loaf of crusty bread and a nice bottle of wine. A picnic by the fire is just the gift for the outdoors fanatic in your family.

Gooey Hot Fudge Sauce

2 cups (12 ounces) semisweet chocolate chips
2 tablespoons butter
½ cup half-and-half
1 tablespoon corn syrup
⅛ teaspoon salt
½ teaspoon vanilla extract

Melt chocolate and butter with half-and-half, corn syrup and salt in heavy 2-quart saucepan over low heat, stirring until smooth. Remove from heat; let stand 10 minutes. Stir in vanilla. Serve warm or pour into clean glass jars and seal tightly. Store up to 6 months in refrigerator. Reheat sauce in double-boiler over hot (not boiling) water before serving, if desired.

Makes about 1½ cups sauce

Pineapple-Peach Salsa

2 cans (20 ounces each) pineapple tidbits in juice, drained
2 cans (15 ounces each) peach slices in juice, drained and chopped
1 can (15 ounces) black beans, rinsed and drained
¼ cup finely chopped red bell pepper
2 jalapeño peppers,* seeded and chopped
2 tablespoons chopped fresh cilantro
2 tablespoons lime juice
2 tablespoons red wine vinegar
½ teaspoon salt
¼ teaspoon ground red pepper
¼ teaspoon garlic powder

*Jalapeño peppers can sting and irritate the skin; wear rubber gloves when handling peppers and do not touch eyes. Wash hands after handling.

1. Combine all ingredients in large bowl; toss to coat.

2. Spoon into 4 labeled 1¾-cup containers. Store in refrigerator up to 2 weeks.

Makes 4 (1¾-cup) containers

Tip: This tropical salsa bursting with fresh flavor is great served with chicken, fish or pork.

Refrigerator Corn Relish

2 cups cut fresh corn (4 ears) *or* 1 (10-ounce) package frozen whole-kernel corn
½ cup vinegar
⅓ cup cold water
1 tablespoon cornstarch
¼ cup chopped onion
¼ cup chopped celery
¼ cup chopped green or red bell pepper
2 tablespoons chopped pimiento
1 teaspoon ground turmeric
½ teaspoon salt
½ teaspoon dry mustard
1¾ teaspoons EQUAL® FOR RECIPES *or* 6 packets EQUAL® sweetener
   or ¼ cup EQUAL® SPOONFUL™

• Cook corn in boiling water until crisp-tender, 5 to 7 minutes; drain and set aside. Combine vinegar, water and cornstarch in large saucepan; stir until cornstarch is dissolved. Add corn, onion, celery, pepper, pimiento, turmeric, salt and mustard. Cook and stir until thickened and bubbly. Cook and stir 2 minutes more. Remove from heat; stir in Equal®. Cool. Cover and store in refrigerator up to 2 weeks. Serve with beef, pork or poultry.

Makes 2½ cups

YULTIDE BREADS & MUFFINS

Sour Cream Coffee Cake with Chocolate and Walnuts

¾ **cup butter, softened**
1½ **cups packed light brown sugar**
 3 **eggs**
 2 **teaspoons vanilla**
 3 **cups all-purpose flour**
 2 **teaspoons baking powder**
 2 **teaspoons ground cinnamon**
1½ **teaspoons baking soda**
 ½ **teaspoon ground nutmeg**
 ¼ **teaspoon salt**
1½ **cups sour cream**
 ½ **cup semisweet chocolate chips**
 ½ **cup chopped walnuts**
   Powdered sugar

Preheat oven to 350°F. Grease and flour 12-cup Bundt pan or 10-inch tube pan. Beat butter in large bowl with electric mixer on medium speed until creamy. Add brown sugar; beat until light and fluffy. Beat in eggs and vanilla until well blended. Combine flour, baking powder, cinnamon, baking soda, nutmeg and salt in large bowl; add to butter mixture on low speed alternately with sour cream, beginning and ending with flour mixture until well blended. Stir in chocolate chips and walnuts. Spoon into prepared pan.

Bake 45 to 50 minutes until wooden pick inserted near center comes out clean. Cool in pan 15 minutes. Remove from pan to wire rack; cool completely. Store tightly covered at room temperature. Sprinkle with powdered sugar before serving.

Makes one 10-inch coffee cake

Maple-Pumpkin-Pecan Twist

1 can (15 ounces) solid pack pumpkin
1 cup water
½ cup shortening
7 to 8 cups all-purpose flour, divided
2 cups pecans, coarsely chopped
½ cup sugar
2 packages active dry yeast
2 teaspoons salt
2 large eggs
2 teaspoons maple flavoring, divided
6 to 8 tablespoons milk
2 cups powdered sugar

1. Heat pumpkin, water and shortening in saucepan over medium heat until shortening is melted and temperature reaches 120° to 130°F. Remove from heat.

2. Combine 4 cups flour, pecans, sugar, yeast and salt in large bowl. Add pumpkin mixture, eggs and 1 teaspoon maple flavoring; beat vigorously 2 minutes. Add remaining flour, ¼ cup at a time, until dough begins to pull away from side of bowl. Turn out dough onto lightly floured work surface; flatten slightly. Knead 10 minutes or until smooth and elastic, adding flour if necessary to prevent sticking. Shape dough into ball. Place in large lightly oiled bowl; turn dough over once to oil surface. Cover with towel; let rise in warm place about 1 hour or until doubled in bulk.

3. Turn out dough onto lightly oiled work surface; divide into four pieces. Shape each piece into 24-inch-long rope. Lightly twist two ropes together. Tuck ends under loaf to prevent untwisting. Place on lightly oiled baking sheet. Repeat with remaining two ropes. Cover with towel; let rise in warm place 45 minutes.

4. Preheat oven to 375°F. Bake 25 minutes or until deep golden brown. Immediately remove bread from baking sheets and cool on wire rack 20 minutes.

5. Combine remaining 1 teaspoon maple flavoring and 6 tablespoons milk in small bowl. Whisk milk mixture and powdered sugar together in medium bowl. If icing is too thick, add remaining milk, 1 teaspoon at a time, to reach desired consistency. Drizzle over loaves in zigzag pattern. *Makes 2 large twists*

Note: Form the twisted ropes into a ring before baking for a pretty, wreath-like presentation.

Cranberry Cheesecake Muffins

1 package (3 ounces) cream cheese, softened
4 tablespoons sugar, divided
1 cup reduced-fat (2%) milk
⅓ cup vegetable oil
1 egg
1 package (about 15 ounces) cranberry quick bread mix

1. Preheat oven to 400°F. Grease 12 muffin cups. Beat cream cheese and 2 tablespoons sugar in small bowl until well blended.

2. Beat milk, oil and egg until blended. Stir in quick bread mix just until dry ingredients are moistened. Fill muffin cups ¼ full with batter. Drop 1 teaspoon cream cheese mixture into center of each cup. Top with remaining batter.

3. Sprinkle batter with remaining 2 tablespoons sugar. Bake 17 to 22 minutes or until golden brown. Cool 5 minutes. Remove from muffin cups to wire rack to cool.

Makes 12 muffins

Star-Of-The-East Fruit Bread

½ cup (1 stick) butter or margarine, softened
1 cup sugar
2 eggs
1 teaspoon vanilla extract
2 cups all-purpose flour
1 teaspoon baking soda
¼ teaspoon salt
1 cup mashed ripe bananas (about 3 medium)
½ cup chopped maraschino cherries, well-drained
1 can (11 ounces) mandarin orange segments, well-drained
½ cup chopped dates or Calimyrna figs
1 cup HERSHEY'S Semi-Sweet Chocolate Chips
Chocolate Drizzle (recipe follows)

1. Heat oven to 350°F. Grease two 8½×4½×2⅝-inch loaf pans.

2. Beat butter and sugar in large bowl until fluffy. Add eggs and vanilla; beat well. Stir together flour, baking soda and salt; add alternately with mashed bananas to butter mixture, blending well. Stir in cherries, orange segments, dates and chocolate chips. Divide batter evenly between prepared pans.

3. Bake 40 to 50 minutes or until golden brown. Cool; remove from pans. Drizzle tops of loaves with Chocolate Drizzle. Store tightly wrapped. *Makes 2 loaves*

Chocolate Drizzle: Combine ½ cup HERSHEY'S Semi-Sweet Chocolate Chips and 2 tablespoons whipping cream in small microwave-safe bowl. Microwave at HIGH (100%) 30 seconds; stir. If necessary, microwave at HIGH an additional 15 seconds stir until chips are melted and mixture is smooth. Makes about ½ cup.

Peach-Almond Scones

2 cups all-purpose flour
¼ cup plus 1 tablespoon sugar, divided
2 teaspoons baking powder
½ teaspoon salt
5 tablespoons margarine or butter
½ cup sliced almonds, lightly toasted and divided
2 tablespoons milk
1 egg
1 can (16 ounces) peaches, drained and finely chopped
½ teaspoon almond extract

Preheat oven to 425°F. Combine flour, ¼ cup sugar, baking powder and salt in large bowl. Cut in margarine with pastry blender or 2 knives until mixture resembles coarse crumbs. Stir in ¼ cup almonds. Lightly beat milk and egg in small bowl. Reserve 2 tablespoons milk mixture; set aside. Stir peaches and almond extract into remaining milk mixture. Stir into flour mixture until soft dough forms.

Turn out dough onto well-floured surface. Gently knead 10 to 12 times. Roll out into 9×6-inch rectangle. Cut dough into 6 (3-inch) squares using floured knife; cut diagonally into halves, forming 12 triangles. Place 2 inches apart on ungreased baking sheets. Brush triangles with reserved milk mixture. Sprinkle with remaining ¼ cup almonds and 1 tablespoon sugar.

Bake 10 to 12 minutes or until golden brown. Remove from baking sheets and cool on wire racks 10 minutes. Serve warm. *Makes 12 scones*

Serving Suggestion: Serve with butter or jelly.

Orchard Fruit Bread

3 cups all-purpose flour or oat flour blend
⅔ cup sugar
1 teaspoon baking soda
2 eggs, beaten
1 carton (8 ounce) lemon lowfat yogurt
⅓ cup vegetable oil
1 teaspoon grated lemon peel
1 can (15 ounces) DEL MONTE® LITE® Fruit Cocktail, drained
½ cup chopped walnuts or pecans

1. Preheat oven to 350°F. Combine flour, sugar and baking soda; mix well.

2. Blend eggs with yogurt, oil and lemon peel. Add dry ingredients along with fruit cocktail and nuts; stir just enough to blend. Spoon into greased 9×5-inch loaf pan.

3. Bake 60 to 70 minutes or until wooden pick inserted into center comes out clean. Let stand in pan 10 minutes. Turn out onto wire rack; cool completely.

Makes 1 loaf

Apricot-Cranberry Holiday Bread

⅔ cup milk
6 tablespoons butter or margarine, softened
2½ to 3 cups all-purpose flour, divided
¼ cup sugar
1 package active dry yeast
¾ teaspoon salt
½ teaspoon ground ginger
½ teaspoon ground nutmeg
2 eggs, divided
½ cup dried apricots, chopped
½ cup dried cranberries, chopped
3 tablespoons orange juice
½ cup pecans, toasted and coarsely chopped
1 teaspoon water

Heat milk and butter in small saucepan over low heat until temperature reaches 120° to 130°F. Combine 1½ cups flour, sugar, yeast, salt, ginger and nutmeg in large bowl. Slowly add heated milk mixture to flour mixture. Add 1 egg; stir with rubber spatula 2 minutes or until blended. Gradually stir in more flour until dough begins to lose its stickiness, about 2 to 3 minutes. Mix apricots, cranberries and orange juice in small microwavable bowl; cover with plastic wrap. Microwave at HIGH 25 to 35 seconds to soften; set aside.

Turn out dough onto floured surface. Knead 5 to 8 minutes or until smooth and elastic; gradually add remaining flour to prevent sticking, if necessary. Drain or blot apricot mixture. Combine apricot mixture and pecans in medium bowl. Flatten dough into ¾-inch-thick rectangle; sprinkle with ⅓ of fruit mixture. Roll up jelly-roll style from short end. Flatten dough; repeat twice using remaining fruit mixture. Continue to knead until blended. Shape dough into ball; place in large greased bowl. Turn dough over. Cover; let rise 1 hour or until doubled in size.

Grease 9-inch round cake or pie pan. Punch down dough; pat into 8-inch circle. Place in pan. Loosely cover with lightly greased sheet of plastic wrap. Let rise 1 hour or until doubled in size.

Preheat oven to 375°F. Beat remaining egg with 1 teaspoon water in small bowl; brush evenly over dough. Bake 30 to 35 minutes or until loaf sounds hollow when tapped. Remove immediately from pan. Cool completely on wire rack.

Makes 12 servings

Greek Spinach-Cheese Rolls

1 loaf (1 pound) frozen bread dough
1 package (10 ounces) frozen chopped spinach, thawed and squeezed dry
¾ cup (3 ounces) crumbled feta cheese
½ cup (2 ounces) shredded reduced-fat Monterey Jack cheese
4 green onions, thinly sliced
1 teaspoon dried dill weed
½ teaspoon garlic powder
½ teaspoon black pepper

1. Thaw bread dough according to package directions. Spray 15 muffin cups with nonstick cooking spray; set aside. Roll out dough on lightly floured surface to 15×9-inch rectangle. (If dough is springy and difficult to roll, cover with plastic wrap and let rest 5 minutes to relax.) Position dough so long edge runs parallel to edge of work surface.

2. Combine spinach, cheeses, green onions, dill weed, garlic powder and pepper in large bowl; mix well.

3. Sprinkle spinach mixture evenly over dough to within 1 inch of long edges. Starting at long edge, roll up snugly, pinching seam closed. Place seam side down; cut roll with serrated knife into 1-inch-wide slices. Place slices cut sides up in prepared muffin cups. Cover with plastic wrap; let stand 30 minutes in warm place until rolls are slightly puffy.

4. Preheat oven to 375°F. Bake 20 to 25 minutes or until golden. Serve warm or at room temperature. Rolls can be stored in refrigerator in airtight container up to 2 days.

Makes 15 rolls

Feta is a classic Greek cheese with a rich, tangy flavor. Traditionally made from sheep's or goat's milk, today feta is often made with cow's milk by large commercial producers. It is often sold in chunks at the deli or in packages of plain or flavored crumbles.

Festive Yule Loaf

2¾ cups all-purpose flour, divided
⅓ cup sugar
1 teaspoon salt
1 package active dry yeast
1 cup milk
½ cup butter or margarine
1 egg
½ cup golden raisins
½ cup chopped candied red and green cherries
½ cup chopped pecans
Vanilla Glaze (recipe follows, optional)

Combine 1½ cups flour, sugar, salt and yeast in large bowl. Heat milk and butter over medium heat until very warm (120° to 130°F). Gradually stir into flour mixture. Add egg. Mix with electric mixer on low speed 1 minute. Beat on high speed 3 minutes, scraping side of bowl frequently. Toss raisins, cherries and pecans with ¼ cup flour in small bowl; stir into yeast mixture. Stir in enough of remaining 1 cup flour to make a soft dough. Turn out onto lightly floured surface. Knead about 10 minutes or until smooth and elastic. Place in greased bowl; turn to grease top of dough. Cover with towel. Let rise in warm, draft-free place about 1 hour or until double in volume.

Punch dough down. Divide in half. Roll out each half on lightly floured surface to form 8-inch circle. Fold in half; press only folded edge firmly. Place on ungreased cookie sheet. Cover with towel. Let rise in warm, draft-free place about 30 minutes or until double in volume.

Preheat oven to 375°F. Bake 20 to 25 minutes until golden brown. Remove from cookie sheet and cool completely on wire rack. Frost with Vanilla Glaze, if desired. Store in airtight containers. *Makes 2 loaves*

Vanilla Glaze: Combine 1 cup sifted powdered sugar, 4 to 5 teaspoons light cream or half-and-half and ½ teaspoon vanilla extract in small bowl; stir until smooth.

Bran and Honey Rye Breadsticks

1 package (¼ ounce) active dry yeast
1 teaspoon sugar
1½ cups warm water (110°F)
3¾ cups all-purpose flour, divided
1 tablespoon honey
1 tablespoon vegetable oil
½ teaspoon salt
1 cup rye flour
½ cup whole bran cereal
Skim milk

1. Dissolve yeast and sugar in warm water in large bowl. Let stand 10 minutes. Add 1 cup all-purpose flour, honey, oil and salt. Beat with electric mixer at medium speed 3 minutes. Stir in rye flour, bran cereal and additional 2 cups all-purpose flour or enough to make moderately stiff dough.

2. Knead dough on lightly floured surface 10 minutes or until smooth and elastic, adding remaining ¾ cup all-purpose flour as necessary to prevent sticking. Place in greased bowl; turn over to grease surface. Cover with damp cloth; let rise in warm place 40 to 45 minutes or until doubled in bulk.

3. Spray 2 baking sheets with nonstick cooking spray. Punch dough down. Divide into 24 equal pieces on lightly floured surface. Roll each piece into an 8-inch rope. Place on prepared baking sheets. Cover with damp cloth; let rise in warm place 30 to 35 minutes or until doubled in bulk.

4. Preheat oven to 375°F. Brush breadsticks with milk. Bake 18 to 20 minutes or until breadsticks are golden brown. Remove from baking sheets. Cool on wire racks.

Makes 24 breadsticks

Holiday Candy Cane Twists

⅓ cup sugar
1 tablespoon ground cinnamon
1 can (11 ounces) refrigerated breadstick dough
3 tablespoons butter or margarine, melted
   Red tube icing (optional)

1. Preheat oven to 350°F. Spray baking sheet with nonstick cooking spray.

2. Combine sugar and cinnamon in small bowl; mix well.

3. Separate dough; roll and stretch each piece of dough into 16-inch rope. Fold rope in half; twist ends together and form into candy cane shape on prepared baking sheet.

4. Brush candy canes with butter; sprinkle with cinnamon-sugar.

5. Bake 12 to 15 minutes or until golden brown. Serve warm, either plain or decorated with red icing as shown in photo. *Makes 8 servings*

Christmas Tree Rolls: Make cinnamon-sugar with green colored sugar instead of granulated sugar. Stretch dough into 16-inch ropes as directed. Cut off ½ inch from 1 end of each rope for tree trunk. Shape ropes into tree shapes on prepared baking sheet; add trunks. Brush with butter and sprinkle with green cinnamon-sugar. Bake as directed. Decorate with red cinnamon candies.

Banana Bran Loaf

1 cup mashed ripe bananas (about 2 large)
½ cup granulated sugar
⅓ cup (5⅓ tablespoons) margarine or butter, melted
⅓ cup fat-free milk
2 egg whites, lightly beaten
1¼ cups all-purpose flour
1 cup QUAKER® Oat Bran hot cereal, uncooked
2 teaspoons baking powder
½ teaspoon baking soda

Heat oven to 350°F. Lightly spray 8×4-inch or 9×5-inch loaf pan with vegetable oil cooking spray or oil lightly. Combine bananas, sugar, melted margarine, milk and egg whites; mix well. Add combined flour, oat bran, baking powder and baking soda, mixing just until moistened. Pour into prepared pan. Bake 55 to 60 minutes or until wooden pick inserted in center comes out clean. Cool 10 minutes; remove from pan. Cool completely on wire rack. *Makes 1 loaf (16 servings)*

Tips: To freeze bread slices, layer waxed paper between each slice of bread. Wrap securely in foil or place in freezer bag. Seal, label and freeze. To reheat, unwrap frozen bread slices and wrap in paper towel. Microwave at HIGH (100% power) about 30 seconds for each slice or until warm.

Cranberry Raisin Nut Bread

1½ cups all-purpose flour
¾ cup packed light brown sugar
1½ teaspoons baking powder
½ teaspoon baking soda
½ teaspoon ground cinnamon
½ teaspoon ground nutmeg
1 cup coarsely chopped fresh or frozen cranberries
½ cup golden raisins
½ cup coarsely chopped pecans
1 tablespoon grated orange peel
2 eggs
¾ cup milk
3 tablespoons butter, melted
1 teaspoon vanilla extract
Cranberry-Orange Spread (recipe follows, optional)

Preheat oven to 350°F. Grease 8½×4½-inch loaf pan.

Combine flour, brown sugar, baking powder, baking soda, cinnamon and nutmeg in large bowl. Stir in cranberries, raisins, pecans and orange peel. Mix eggs, milk, butter and vanilla in small bowl until combined; stir into flour mixture just until moistened. Spoon into prepared pan.

Bake 55 to 60 minutes or until wooden toothpick inserted in center comes out clean. Cool in pan 15 minutes. Remove from pan and cool completely on wire rack. Store tightly wrapped in plastic wrap at room temperature. Serve slices with Cranberry-Orange Spread, if desired. *Makes 1 loaf*

Cranberry-Orange Spread

1 package (8 ounces) cream cheese, softened
1 package (3 ounces) cream cheese, softened
1 container (12 ounces) cranberry-orange sauce
¾ cup chopped pecans

Combine cream cheese and cranberry-orange sauce in small bowl; stir until blended. Stir in pecans. Store in refrigerator. *Makes about 3 cups spread*

Cranberry Raisin Nut Bread

Blueberry White Chip Muffins

       2 cups all-purpose flour
     ½ cup granulated sugar
     ¼ cup packed brown sugar
    2½ teaspoons baking powder
     ½ teaspoon salt
     ¾ cup milk
       1 large egg, lightly beaten
     ¼ cup butter or margarine, melted
     ½ teaspoon grated lemon peel
       2 cups (12-ounce package) NESTLÉ® TOLL HOUSE® Premier White Morsels,
         divided
    1½ cups fresh or frozen blueberries
       Streusel Topping (recipe follows)

PREHEAT oven to 375°F. Paper-line 18 muffin cups.

COMBINE flour, granulated sugar, brown sugar, baking powder and salt in large bowl. Stir in milk, egg, butter and lemon peel. Stir in *1½ cups* morsels and blueberries. Spoon into prepared muffin cups, filling almost full. Sprinkle with Streusel Topping.

BAKE for 22 to 25 minutes or until wooden pick inserted in center comes out clean. Cool in pans for 5 minutes; remove to wire racks to cool slightly.

PLACE *remaining* morsels in small, *heavy-duty* resealable plastic food storage bag. Microwave on MEDIUM-HIGH (70%) power for 30 seconds; knead. Microwave at additional 10- to 20-second intervals, kneading until smooth. Cut tiny corner from bag; squeeze to drizzle over muffins. Serve warm.   *Makes 18 muffins*

Streusel Topping: **COMBINE** ⅓ cup granulated sugar, ¼ cup all-purpose flour and ¼ teaspoon ground cinnamon in small bowl. Cut in 3 tablespoons butter or margarine with pastry blender or two knives until mixture resembles coarse crumbs.

Blueberry White Chip Muffins

Holiday Stollen

1½ cups unsalted butter, softened
 4 egg yolks
 ½ cup granulated sugar
 1 teaspoon salt
   Grated peel from 1 lemon
   Grated peel from 1 orange
 1 teaspoon vanilla
2½ cups hot milk (120° to 130°F)
 8 to 8½ cups all-purpose flour, divided
 2 packages active dry yeast
 ½ cup golden raisins
 ½ cup candied orange peel
 ½ cup candied lemon peel
 ½ cup chopped red candied cherries
 ½ cup chopped green candied cherries
 ½ cup chopped almonds
 1 egg, beaten
   Powdered sugar

Beat butter, egg yolks, granulated sugar, salt, lemon peel, orange peel and vanilla in large bowl until light and fluffy. Slowly add milk; mix thoroughly. Add 2 cups flour and yeast; mix well. When mixture is smooth, add enough remaining flour, ½ cup at a time, until dough forms and can be lifted out of bowl. Lightly flour work surface; knead dough until smooth and elastic, about 10 minutes. Mix raisins, candied orange and lemon peels, cherries and almonds in medium bowl; knead fruit mixture into dough.

Place dough in greased bowl, cover with plastic wrap and let rise in warm place about 1 hour or until doubled in bulk.

Grease 2 large baking sheets. Turn dough out onto floured work surface. Divide dough in half. Place one half back in bowl; cover and set aside. Cut remaining half into thirds. Roll each third into 12-inch rope. Place on prepared baking sheet. Braid ropes together. Repeat procedure with remaining dough.

Brush beaten egg on braids. Let braids stand at room temperature about 1 hour or until doubled in bulk.

Preheat oven to 350°F. Bake braids about 45 minutes or until golden brown and sound hollow when tapped. Remove to wire rack to cool. Sprinkle with powdered sugar before serving. *Makes 2 braided loaves*

Pumpkin Cranberry Bread

    3 cups all-purpose flour
    1 tablespoon plus 2 teaspoons pumpkin pie spice
    2 teaspoons baking soda
 1½ teaspoons salt
    3 cups granulated sugar
    1 can (15 ounces) LIBBY'S® 100% Pure Pumpkin
    4 large eggs
    1 cup vegetable oil
  ½ cup orange juice or water
    1 cup sweetened dried, fresh or frozen cranberries

PREHEAT oven to 350°F. Grease and flour two 9×5-inch loaf pans.

COMBINE flour, pumpkin pie spice, baking soda and salt in large bowl. Combine sugar, pumpkin, eggs, vegetable oil and orange juice in large mixer bowl; beat until just blended. Add pumpkin mixture to flour mixture; stir just until moistened. Fold in cranberries. Spoon batter into prepared loaf pans.

BAKE for 60 to 65 minutes or until wooden pick inserted in center comes out clean. Cool in pans on wire racks for 10 minutes; remove to wire racks to cool completely.

Makes 2 loaves

For Three 8×4-inch Loaf Pans: **PREPARE** as above. Bake for 55 to 60 minutes.

For Five or Six 5×3-inch Mini-Loaf Pans: **PREPARE** as above. Bake for 50 to 55 minutes.

The batter for quick breads and muffins should be mixed very gently, and only until the dry ingredients are moistened. (Any lumps will disappear during baking.) Overmixing or overbeating will result in tough, dense breads or muffins.

Pumpkin Cranberry Bread

White Chocolate Chunk Muffins

2½ cups all-purpose flour
1 cup packed brown sugar
⅓ cup unsweetened cocoa powder
2 teaspoons baking soda
½ teaspoon salt
1⅓ cups buttermilk
6 tablespoons butter, melted
2 eggs, beaten
1½ teaspoons vanilla
1½ cups chopped white chocolate

Preheat oven to 400°F. Grease 12 (3½-inch) large muffin cups. Combine flour, sugar, cocoa, baking soda and salt in large bowl. Combine buttermilk, butter, eggs and vanilla in small bowl until blended. Stir into flour mixture just until moistened. Fold in white chocolate. Spoon into prepared muffin cups, filling half full.

Bake 25 to 30 minutes or until wooden pick inserted in centers comes out clean. Cool in pan on wire rack 5 minutes. Remove from pan. Cool on wire rack 10 minutes. Serve warm or cool completely.   *Makes 12 jumbo muffins*

Apple Cheddar Scones

1½ cups unsifted all-purpose flour
½ cup toasted wheat germ
3 tablespoons sugar
2 teaspoons baking powder
½ teaspoon salt
2 tablespoons butter
1 small Washington Rome apple, cored and chopped
¼ cup shredded Cheddar cheese
1 large egg white
½ cup low fat (1%) milk

1. Heat oven to 400°F. Grease 8-inch round cake pan. In medium bowl, combine flour, wheat germ, sugar, baking powder and salt. With two knives or pastry blender, cut in butter until the size of coarse crumbs. Toss apple and cheese in flour mixture.

2. Beat together egg white and milk until well combined. Add to flour mixture, mixing with fork until dough forms. Turn dough out onto lightly floured surface and knead 6 times.

3. Spread dough evenly in cake pan and score deeply with knife into 6 wedges. Bake 25 to 30 minutes or until top springs back when gently pressed. Let stand 5 minutes; remove from pan. Cool before serving.   *Makes 6 scones*

*Favorite recipe from **Washington Apple Commission***

White Chocolate Chunk Muffins

Cherry Eggnog Quick Bread

2½ cups all-purpose flour
¾ cup sugar
1 tablespoon baking powder
½ teaspoon ground nutmeg
1¼ cups prepared dairy eggnog
6 tablespoons butter, melted and cooled
2 eggs, lightly beaten
1 teaspoon vanilla
½ cup chopped pecans
½ cup chopped candied red cherries

Preheat oven to 350°F. Grease three 5½×3-inch mini-loaf pans. Combine flour, sugar, baking powder and nutmeg in large bowl. Stir eggnog, melted butter, eggs and vanilla in medium bowl until well blended. Add eggnog mixture to flour mixture; mix just until moistened. Stir in pecans and cherries. Spoon into prepared pans.

Bake 35 to 40 minutes or until wooden toothpick inserted in centers comes out clean. Cool in pans 15 minutes. Remove from pans and cool completely on wire rack. Store tightly wrapped in plastic wrap at room temperature.   *Makes 3 mini loaves*

Holiday Pumpkin Muffins

2½ cups all-purpose flour
1 cup packed light brown sugar
1 tablespoon baking powder
1 teaspoon ground cinnamon
½ teaspoon ground nutmeg
½ teaspoon ground ginger
¼ teaspoon salt
1 cup solid pack pumpkin (not pumpkin pie filling)
¾ cup milk
2 eggs
6 tablespoons butter, melted
⅔ cup roasted, salted pepitas (pumpkin seeds), divided
½ cup golden raisins

Preheat oven to 400°F. Grease or paper-line 18 (2¾-inch) muffin cups. Combine flour, brown sugar, baking powder, cinnamon, nutmeg, ginger and salt in large bowl. Stir pumpkin, milk, eggs and melted butter in medium bowl until well blended. Stir pumpkin mixture into flour mixture. Mix just until all ingredients are moistened. Stir in ⅓ cup pepitas and raisins. Spoon into prepared muffin cups, filling ⅔ full. Sprinkle remaining pepitas over muffin batter.

Bake 15 to 18 minutes or until wooden pick inserted in center comes out clean. Cool in pans 10 minutes. Remove from pans and cool completely on wire racks. Store in airtight container.   *Makes 18 muffins*

Pumpkin-Ginger Scones

½ **cup sugar, divided**
2 **cups all-purpose flour**
2 **teaspoons baking powder**
1 **teaspoon ground cinnamon**
½ **teaspoon baking soda**
½ **teaspoon salt**
5 **tablespoons butter, divided**
1 **egg**
½ **cup solid pack pumpkin**
¼ **cup sour cream**
½ **teaspoon grated fresh ginger** *or* **2 tablespoons finely chopped crystallized ginger**

Preheat oven to 425°F.

Reserve 1 tablespoon sugar. Combine remaining sugar, flour, baking powder, cinnamon, baking soda and salt in large bowl. Cut in 4 tablespoons butter with pastry blender until mixture resembles coarse crumbs. Beat egg in small bowl. Add pumpkin, sour cream and ginger; beat until well combined. Add pumpkin mixture to flour mixture; stir until mixture forms soft dough that leaves side of bowl.

Turn dough out onto well-floured surface. Knead 10 times. Roll dough using floured rolling pin into 9×6-inch rectangle. Cut dough into 6 (3-inch) squares. Cut each square diagonally in half, making 12 triangles. Place triangles, 2 inches apart, on ungreased baking sheets. Melt remaining 1 tablespoon butter. Brush tops of triangles with butter and sprinkle with reserved sugar.

Bake 10 to 12 minutes or until golden brown. Cool 10 minutes on wire racks. Serve warm.

Makes 12 scones

Avoid purchasing ginger that has wrinkled and/or cracked skin, as this is a sign that the ginger is old and dried out. Unpeeled gingerroot should be stored in a sealed plastic bag in the refrigerator for up to 3 weeks.

Tex-Mex Quick Bread

1½ cups all-purpose flour
1 cup (4 ounces) shredded Monterey Jack cheese
½ cup cornmeal
½ cup sun-dried tomatoes, coarsely chopped
1 can (4¼ ounces) black olives, drained and chopped
¼ cup sugar
1½ teaspoons baking powder
1 teaspoon baking soda
1 cup milk
1 can (4½ ounces) green chilies, drained and chopped
¼ cup olive oil
1 large egg, beaten

1. Preheat oven to 325°F. Grease 9×5-inch loaf pan or four 5×3-inch loaf pans.

2. Combine flour, cheese, cornmeal, tomatoes, olives, sugar, baking powder and baking soda in large bowl. Combine remaining ingredients in small bowl. Add to flour mixture; stir just until combined. Pour into prepared pan.

3. Bake 9×5-inch loaf 45 minutes and 5×3-inch loaves 30 minutes or until toothpick inserted near center of loaf comes out clean. Cool in pan 15 minutes. Remove from pan and cool on wire rack. *Makes 1 large loaf or 4 small loaves*

Sweet Potato Biscuits

2½ cups all-purpose flour
¼ cup packed brown sugar
1 tablespoon baking powder
¾ teaspoon salt
¾ teaspoon ground cinnamon
¼ teaspoon ground ginger
¼ teaspoon ground allspice
½ cup vegetable shortening
½ cup chopped pecans
¾ cup mashed canned sweet potatoes
½ cup milk

Preheat oven to 450°F. Combine flour, sugar, baking powder, salt and spices in large bowl. Cut in shortening with pastry blender or 2 knives until mixture resembles coarse crumbs. Stir in pecans. Combine sweet potatoes and milk in medium bowl with wire whisk until smooth. Make well in center of flour mixture. Add sweet potato mixture; stir until mixture forms soft dough that clings together and forms a ball. Turn out dough onto well-floured surface. Knead dough gently 10 to 12 times. Roll or pat dough to ½-inch thickness. Cut out dough with floured 2½-inch biscuit cutter. Place biscuits 2 inches apart on ungreased baking sheet. Bake 12 to 14 minutes or until golden brown. Serve warm. *Makes about 12 biscuits*

Cherry-Coconut-Cheese Coffee Cake

2½ **cups all-purpose flour**
¾ **cup sugar**
½ **teaspoon baking powder**
½ **teaspoon baking soda**
 2 **packages (3 ounces each) cream cheese, softened, divided**
¾ **cup milk**
 2 **tablespoons vegetable oil**
 2 **eggs, divided**
 1 **teaspoon vanilla**
½ **cup flaked coconut**
¾ **cup cherry preserves**
 2 **tablespoons margarine or butter**

Preheat oven to 350°F. Grease and flour 9-inch springform pan. Combine flour and sugar in large bowl. Reserve ½ cup flour mixture; set aside. Stir baking powder and baking soda into remaining flour mixture. Cut in 1 package cream cheese with pastry blender or 2 knives until mixture resembles coarse crumbs; set aside.

Combine milk, oil and 1 egg in medium bowl. Add to cream cheese mixture; stir just until moistened. Spread batter on bottom and 1 inch up side of prepared pan. Combine remaining package cream cheese, remaining egg and vanilla in small bowl; stir until smooth. Pour over batter, spreading to within 1 inch of edge. Sprinkle coconut over cream cheese mixture. Spoon preserves evenly over coconut.

Cut margarine into reserved flour mixture with pastry blender or 2 knives until mixture resembles coarse crumbs. Sprinkle over preserves. Bake 55 to 60 minutes or until brown and toothpick inserted into crust comes out clean. Cool in pan on wire rack 15 minutes. Remove side of pan; serve warm. *Makes 10 servings*

Cherry-Coconut-Cheese Coffee Cake

Caramel Pecan Spice Cakes

Cake

    1 package DUNCAN HINES® Moist Deluxe® Spice Cake Mix
    1 package (4-serving size) vanilla instant pudding and pie filling mix
    4 eggs
    1 cup water
    ⅓ cup vegetable oil
    1½ cups pecan pieces, toasted and finely chopped

Caramel Glaze

    3 tablespoons butter or margarine
    3 tablespoons brown sugar
    3 tablespoons granulated sugar
    3 tablespoons whipping cream
    ½ cup confectioners' sugar
    ¼ teaspoon vanilla extract
    Pecan halves, for garnish
    Maraschino cherry halves, for garnish

1. Preheat oven to 350°F. Grease and flour two 8½×4½×2½-inch loaf pans.

2. For cake, combine cake mix, pudding mix, eggs, water and oil in large bowl. Beat at medium speed with electric mixer for 2 minutes. Stir in toasted pecans. Pour batter into pans. Bake at 350°F for 55 to 60 minutes or until toothpick inserted in center comes out clean. Cool in pans 15 minutes. Loosen loaves from pans. Invert onto cooling rack. Turn right sides up. Cool completely.

3. For caramel glaze, combine butter, brown sugar, granulated sugar and whipping cream in small heavy saucepan. Bring to a boil on medium heat; boil 1 minute. Remove from heat; cool 20 minutes. Add confectioners' sugar and vanilla extract; blend with wooden spoon until smooth and thick. Spread evenly on cooled loaves. Garnish with pecan halves and maraschino cherry halves before glaze sets.

Makes 2 loaves (24 slices)

COOKIE TIN EXPRESS

Jolly Peanut Butter Gingerbread Cookies

1⅔ cups (10-ounce package) REESE'S® Peanut Butter Chips
¾ cup (1½ sticks) butter or margarine, softened
1 cup packed light brown sugar
1 cup dark corn syrup
2 eggs
5 cups all-purpose flour
1 teaspoon baking soda
½ teaspoon ground cinnamon
¼ teaspoon ground ginger
¼ teaspoon salt

1. Place peanut butter chips in small microwave-safe bowl. Microwave at HIGH (100%) 1 to 2 minutes or until chips are melted when stirred. Beat melted peanut butter chips and butter in large bowl until well blended. Add brown sugar, corn syrup and eggs; beat until fluffy.

2. Stir together flour, baking soda, cinnamon, ginger and salt. Add half of flour mixture to butter mixture; beat on low speed of mixer until smooth. With wooden spoon, stir in remaining flour mixture until well blended. Divide into thirds; wrap each in plastic wrap. Refrigerate at least 1 hour or until dough is firm enough to roll.

3. Heat oven to 325°F.

4. Roll 1 dough portion at a time to ⅛-inch thickness on lightly floured surface; with floured cookie cutters, cut into holiday shapes. Place on ungreased cookie sheet.

5. Bake 10 to 12 minutes or until set and lightly browned. Cool slightly; remove from cookie sheet to wire rack. Cool completely. Frost and decorate as desired.

Makes about 6 dozen cookies

Jolly Peanut Butter Gingerbread Cookies

Lemony Butter Cookies

½ **cup butter, softened**
½ **cup sugar**
1 **egg**
1½ **cups all-purpose flour**
2 **tablespoons fresh lemon juice**
1 **teaspoon grated lemon peel**
½ **teaspoon baking powder**
⅛ **teaspoon salt**
  Additional sugar

Beat butter and sugar in large bowl with electric mixer at medium speed until creamy. Beat in egg until light and fluffy. Mix in flour, lemon juice and peel, baking powder and salt. Cover; refrigerate about 2 hours or until firm.

Preheat oven to 350°F. Roll out dough, a small portion at a time, on well-floured surface to ¼-inch thickness. (Keep remaining dough in refrigerator.) Cut with 3-inch round or fluted cookie cutter. Transfer to ungreased cookie sheets. Sprinkle with sugar.

Bake 8 to 10 minutes or until edges are lightly browned. Cool 1 minute on cookie sheets. Remove to wire racks; cool completely. *Makes about 2½ dozen cookies*

Chocolate-Dipped Almond Horns

1½ **cups powdered sugar**
1 **cup butter, softened**
2 **egg yolks**
1½ **teaspoons vanilla**
2¼ **cups all-purpose flour**
½ **cup ground almonds**
1 **teaspoon cream of tartar**
1 **teaspoon baking soda**
2 **cups semisweet chocolate chips, melted**
  Powdered sugar

1. Preheat oven to 325°F. In large bowl, combine powdered sugar and butter. Beat at medium speed, scraping bowl often, until creamy, 1 to 2 minutes. Add egg yolks and vanilla; continue beating until well blended, 1 to 2 minutes. Reduce speed to low. Add flour, almonds, cream of tartar and baking soda. Continue beating, scraping bowl often, until well mixed, 1 to 2 minutes.

2. Shape into 1-inch balls. Roll balls into 2½-inch ropes; shape into crescents. Place 2 inches apart on ungreased cookie sheets.

3. Bake 8 to 10 minutes or until set. (Cookies do not brown.) Cool completely.

4. Dip half of each cookie into chocolate; sprinkle remaining half with powdered sugar. Refrigerate until set. *Makes about 3 dozen cookies*

Chunky Chocolate Chip Peanut Butter Cookies

1¼ cups all-purpose flour
½ teaspoon baking soda
½ teaspoon ground cinnamon
½ teaspoon salt
¾ cup (1½ sticks) butter or margarine, softened
½ cup packed brown sugar
½ cup granulated sugar
½ cup creamy peanut butter
1 large egg
1 teaspoon vanilla extract
2 cups (12-ounce package) NESTLÉ® TOLL HOUSE® Semi-Sweet
   Chocolate Morsels
½ cup coarsely chopped peanuts

PREHEAT oven to 375°F.

COMBINE flour, baking soda, cinnamon and salt in small bowl. Beat butter, brown sugar, granulated sugar and peanut butter in large mixer bowl until creamy. Beat in egg and vanilla extract. Gradually beat in flour mixture. Stir in morsels and peanuts.

DROP dough by rounded tablespoon onto ungreased baking sheets. Press down slightly to flatten into 2-inch circles.

BAKE for 7 to 10 minutes or until edges are set but centers are still soft. Cool on baking sheets for 4 minutes; remove to wire racks to cool completely.

Makes about 3 dozen cookies

Apple Crumb Squares

2 cups QUAKER® Oats (quick or old fashioned, uncooked)
1½ cups all-purpose flour
1 cup packed brown sugar
¾ cup (12 tablespoons) butter or margarine, melted
1 teaspoon ground cinnamon
½ teaspoon baking soda
½ teaspoon salt (optional)
¼ teaspoon ground nutmeg
1 cup applesauce
½ cup chopped nuts

Preheat oven to 350°F. In large bowl, combine all ingredients except applesauce and nuts; mix until crumbly. Reserve 1 cup oats mixture. Press remaining mixture on bottom of greased 13×9-inch metal baking pan. Bake 13 to 15 minutes; cool. Spread applesauce over partially baked crust. Sprinkle reserved 1 cup oats mixture over top; sprinkle with nuts. Bake 13 to 15 minutes or until golden brown. Cool in pan on wire rack; cut into 2-inch squares. *Makes about 2 dozen bars*

Festive Fruited White Chip Blondies

½ cup (1 stick) butter or margarine
1⅔ cups (10-ounce package) HERSHEY.S Premier White Chips, divided
2 eggs
¼ cup granulated sugar
1¼ cups all-purpose flour
⅓ cup orange juice
¾ cup cranberries, chopped
¼ cup chopped dried apricots
½ cup coarsely chopped nuts
¼ cup packed light brown sugar

1. Heat oven to 325°F. Grease and flour 9-inch square baking pan.

2. Melt butter in medium saucepan; stir in 1 cup white chips. In large bowl, beat eggs until foamy. Add granulated sugar; beat until thick and pale yellow in color. Add flour, orange juice and white chip mixture; beat just until combined. Spread one-half of batter, about 1¼ cups, into prepared pan.

3. Bake 15 minutes or until edges are lightly browned; remove from oven.

4. Stir cranberries, apricots and remaining ⅔ cup white chips into remaining one-half of batter; spread over top of hot baked mixture. Stir together nuts and brown sugar; sprinkle over top.

5. Bake 25 to 30 minutes or until edges are lightly browned. Cool completely in pan on wire rack. Cut into bars. *Makes about 16 bars*

Homemade Coconut Macaroons

3 egg whites
¼ teaspoon cream of tartar
⅛ teaspoon salt
¾ cup sugar
2¼ cups shredded coconut, toasted*
1 teaspoon vanilla

To toast coconut, spread evenly on cookie sheet. Toast in preheated 350°F oven 7 minutes. Stir and toast 1 to 2 minutes more or until light golden brown.

Preheat oven to 325°F. Line cookie sheets with parchment paper or foil. Beat egg whites, cream of tartar and salt in large bowl with electric mixer until soft peaks form. Beat in sugar, 1 tablespoon at a time, until egg whites are stiff and shiny. Fold in coconut and vanilla. Drop tablespoonfuls of dough 4 inches apart onto prepared cookie sheets; spread each into 3-inch circles with back of spoon.

Bake 18 to 22 minutes or until light brown. Cool 1 minute on cookie sheets. Remove to wire racks; cool completely. Store in airtight container.

Makes about 2 dozen cookies

Oatmeal Toffee Cookies

1 cup (2 sticks) butter or margarine, softened
2 eggs
2 cups packed light brown sugar
2 teaspoons vanilla extract
1¾ cups all-purpose flour
1 teaspoon baking soda
1 teaspoon ground cinnamon
½ teaspoon salt
3 cups quick-cooking oats
1¾ cups (10-ounce package) HEATH® Almond Toffee Bits or SKOR® English
    Toffee Bits
1 cup MOUNDS® Coconut Flakes (optional)

1. Heat oven to 375°F. Lightly grease cookie sheet. Beat butter, eggs, brown sugar and vanilla until well blended. Add flour, baking soda, cinnamon and salt; beat until blended.

2. Stir in oats, toffee and coconut, if desired, with spoon. Drop dough by rounded teaspoons about 2 inches apart onto prepared sheet.

3. Bake 8 to 10 minutes or until edges are lightly browned. Cool 1 minute; remove to wire rack.   *Makes about 4 dozen cookies*

Elephant Ears

1 package (17¼ ounces) frozen puff pastry, thawed according to
    package directions
1 egg, beaten
¼ cup sugar, divided
2 squares (1 ounce each) semisweet chocolate

Preheat oven to 375°F. Grease cookie sheets; sprinkle lightly with water. Roll one sheet of pastry to 12×10-inch rectangle. Brush with egg; sprinkle with 1 tablespoon sugar. Tightly roll up 10-inch sides, meeting in center. Brush center with egg and seal rolls tightly together; turn over. Cut into ⅜-inch-thick slices. Place slices on prepared cookie sheets. Sprinkle with 1 tablespoon sugar. Repeat with remaining pastry, egg and sugar. Bake 16 to 18 minutes until golden brown. Remove to wire racks; cool completely.

Melt chocolate in small saucepan over low heat, stirring constantly. Remove from heat. Spread bottoms of cookies with chocolate. Place on wire rack, chocolate side up. Let stand until chocolate is set. Store between layers of waxed paper in airtight containers.   *Makes about 4 dozen cookies*

Snowmen

1 package (20 ounces) refrigerated chocolate chip cookie dough
1½ cups sifted powdered sugar
2 tablespoons milk
Candy corn, gumdrops, chocolate chips, licorice and other assorted small candies

1. Preheat oven to 375°F. Cut dough into 12 equal sections. Divide each section into 3 balls: large, medium and small for each snowman. For each snowman, place 3 balls in row, ¼ inch apart, on ungreased cookie sheet.

2. Bake 10 to 12 minutes or until edges are very lightly browned. Cool 4 minutes on cookie sheets. Remove to wire racks; cool completely.

3. Mix powdered sugar and milk in medium bowl until smooth. Pour over cookies. Let cookies stand 20 minutes or until set. Decorate with assorted candies to create snowman faces, hats and arms.

Makes 1 dozen cookies

Chocolate-Dipped Orange Logs

3¼ cups all-purpose flour
⅓ teaspoon salt
1 cup butter, softened
1 cup sugar
2 eggs
1½ teaspoons grated orange peel
1 teaspoon vanilla
1 package (12 ounces) semisweet chocolate chips
1½ cups pecan pieces, finely chopped

Combine flour and salt in medium bowl. Beat butter in large bowl with electric mixer at medium speed until smooth. Gradually beat in sugar; beat at high speed until light and fluffy. Beat in eggs, 1 at a time, blending well after each addition. Beat in orange peel and vanilla until blended. Gradually stir in flour mixture until blended. (Dough will be crumbly.) Gather dough together and press gently to form ball. Flatten into disc; wrap in plastic wrap and refrigerate 2 hours or until firm.

Preheat oven to 350°F. Shape dough into 1-inch balls. Roll balls on flat surface to form 3-inch logs about ½ inch thick. Place logs 1 inch apart on ungreased cookie sheets. Bake 17 minutes or until bottoms are golden brown. (Cookies will feel soft and look white on top; they will become crisp when cool.) Cool completely on wire racks.

Melt chocolate chips in top of double boiler over hot, not boiling, water. Place pecans on sheet of waxed paper. Dip one end of each cookie in chocolate, shaking off excess. Roll chocolate-covered ends in pecans. Place on waxed paper-lined cookie sheets and let stand until chocolate is set, or refrigerate about 5 minutes to set chocolate. Store in airtight container.

Makes about 3 dozen cookies

Chocolate Reindeer

1 cup butter, softened
1 cup granulated sugar
1 egg
1 teaspoon vanilla
2 ounces semisweet chocolate, melted
2¼ cups all-purpose flour
1 teaspoon baking powder
¼ teaspoon salt
Royal Icing (recipe follows)
Assorted food colors
Assorted small candies

1. Beat butter and sugar in large bowl at high speed of electric mixer until fluffy. Beat in egg and vanilla. Add melted chocolate; mix well. Add flour, baking powder and salt; mix well. Divide dough in half; wrap each half in plastic wrap and refrigerate 2 hours or until firm.

2. Preheat oven to 325°F. Grease 2 cookie sheets. Roll out half of dough on well-floured surface to ¼-inch thickness. Cut out with reindeer cookie cutter. Place 2 inches apart on prepared cookie sheets. Chill 10 minutes.

3. Bake 13 to 15 minutes or until set. Cool completely on cookie sheets. Repeat steps with remaining dough.

4. Prepare Royal Icing. Tint with food colors as desired. Pipe icing on reindeer and decorate with small candies. For best results, let cookies dry overnight uncovered before storing in airtight container at room temperature.

Makes 16 (4-inch) cookies

Royal Icing

2 to 3 large egg whites*
2 to 4 cups powdered sugar
1 tablespoon lemon juice
Assorted food colors

*Use only grade A clean, uncracked eggs.

Beat 2 egg whites in medium bowl with electric mixer until peaks just begin to hold their shape. Add 2 cups powdered sugar and lemon juice; beat for 1 minute. If consistency is too thin for piping, gradually add more sugar until desired result is achieved; if it is too thick, add another egg white. Divide icing among several small bowls and tint to desired colors. Keep bowls tightly covered until ready to use.

Chocolate Reindeer

Tiny Mini Kisses Peanut Blossoms

¾ cup REESE'S® Creamy Peanut Butter
½ cup shortening
⅓ cup granulated sugar
⅓ cup packed light brown sugar
1 egg
3 tablespoons milk
1 teaspoon vanilla extract
1½ cups all-purpose flour
½ teaspoon baking soda
½ teaspoon salt
Granulated sugar
HERSHEY'S MINI KISSES™ Semi-Sweet *or* Milk Chocolates

1. Heat oven to 350°F.

2. Beat peanut butter and shortening in large bowl with mixer until well mixed. Add ⅓ cup granulated sugar and brown sugar; beat well. Add egg, milk and vanilla; beat until fluffy. Stir together flour, baking soda and salt; gradually add to peanut butter mixture, beating until blended. Shape into ½-inch balls. Roll in granulated sugar; place on ungreased cookie sheet.

3. Bake 5 to 6 minutes or until set. Immediately press Mini Kiss™ into center of each cookie. Transfer cookies to wire rack.   *Makes about 14 dozen cookies*

Variation: For larger cookies, shape dough into 1-inch balls. Roll in granulated sugar. Place on ungreased cookie sheet. Bake 10 minutes or until set. Immediately place 3 Mini Kisses™ in center of each cookie, pressing down slightly. Remove from cookie sheet to wire rack. Cool completely.

Snickerdoodles

3 tablespoons sugar
1 teaspoon ground cinnamon
1 package DUNCAN HINES® Moist Deluxe® Classic Yellow Cake Mix
2 eggs
¼ cup vegetable oil

1. Preheat oven to 375°F. Grease baking sheets. Place sheets of foil on countertop for cooling cookies.

2. Combine sugar and cinnamon in small bowl.

3. Combine cake mix, eggs and oil in large bowl. Stir until well blended. Shape dough into 1-inch balls. Roll in cinnamon-sugar mixture. Place balls 2 inches apart on baking sheets. Flatten balls with bottom of glass.

4. Bake at 375°F for 8 to 9 minutes or until set. Cool 1 minute on baking sheets. Remove to foil to cool completely.   *Makes about 3 dozen cookies*

Santa's Favorite Brownies

1 cup (6 ounces) milk chocolate chips
½ cup butter
¾ cup granulated sugar
2 eggs
1 teaspoon vanilla
1¼ cups all-purpose flour
3 tablespoons unsweetened cocoa powder
1 teaspoon baking powder
½ teaspoon salt
½ cup chopped walnuts
Buttercream Frosting (recipe follows, optional)
Small jelly beans, icing gels and colored sugar for decoration (optional)

Preheat oven to 350°F. Grease 9-inch square baking pan. Melt chocolate and butter with granulated sugar in medium saucepan over low heat, stirring constantly. Pour into large bowl; add eggs and vanilla. Beat with electric mixer until well blended. Stir in flour, cocoa, baking powder and salt; blend well. Fold in walnuts. Spread in prepared pan.

Bake 25 to 30 minutes or until wooden toothpick inserted in center comes out clean. Place pan on wire rack; cool completely. Frost with Buttercream Frosting, if desired. Cut into squares. Decorate with jelly beans, icing gels and colored sugar, if desired. Store in airtight container. *Makes 16 brownies*

Buttercream Frosting

3 cups powdered sugar, sifted
½ cup butter or margarine, softened
3 to 4 tablespoons milk, divided
½ teaspoon vanilla extract

Combine powdered sugar, butter, 2 tablespoons milk and vanilla in large bowl. Beat with electric mixer on low speed until blended. Beat on high speed until light and fluffy, adding more milk, 1 teaspoon at a time, as needed for good spreading consistency. *Makes about 1½ cups frosting*

Santa's Favorite Brownies

Peanut Butter Chip Tassies

1 package (3 ounces) cream cheese, softened
½ cup (1 stick) butter, softened
1 cup all-purpose flour
1 egg, slightly beaten
½ cup sugar
2 tablespoons butter, melted
¼ teaspoon lemon juice
¼ teaspoon vanilla extract
1 cup REESE'S® Peanut Butter Chips, chopped*
6 red candied cherries, quartered (optional)

*Do not chop peanut butter chips in food processor or blender.

1. Beat cream cheese and ½ cup butter in medium bowl; stir in flour. Cover; refrigerate about one hour or until dough is firm. Shape into 24 one-inch balls; place each ball into ungreased, small muffin cups (1¾ inches in diameter). Press dough evenly against bottom and sides of each cup.

2. Heat oven to 350°F. Combine egg, sugar, melted butter, lemon juice and vanilla in medium bowl; stir until smooth. Add chopped peanut butter chips. Fill muffin cups ¾ full with mixture.

3. Bake 20 to 25 minutes or until filling is set and lightly browned. Cool completely; remove from pan to wire rack. Garnish with candied cherries, if desired.

Makes about 2 dozen

Honey Spice Balls

½ cup butter, softened
½ cup packed brown sugar
1 egg
1 tablespoon honey
1 teaspoon vanilla extract
2 cups all-purpose flour
½ teaspoon baking powder
½ teaspoon ground cinnamon
¼ teaspoon ground nutmeg
Uncooked quick oats

Preheat oven to 350°F. Grease cookie sheets. Beat butter and brown sugar in large bowl with electric mixer until creamy. Add egg, honey and vanilla; beat until light and fluffy. Stir in flour, baking powder, cinnamon and nutmeg until well blended. Shape tablespoonfuls of dough into balls; roll in oats. Place 2 inches apart on prepared cookie sheets.

Bake 15 to 18 minutes until cookie tops crack slightly. Cool 1 minute on cookie sheets. Remove to wire racks; cool completely. Store in airtight container.

Makes about 2½ dozen cookies

Cashew-Lemon Shortbread Cookies

½ **cup roasted cashews**
1 **cup butter, softened**
½ **cup sugar**
2 **teaspoons lemon extract**
1 **teaspoon vanilla**
2 **cups all-purpose flour**
   Additional sugar

1. Preheat oven to 325°F. Place cashews in food processor; process until finely ground. Add butter, sugar, lemon extract and vanilla; process until well blended. Add flour; process using on/off pulses until dough is well blended and begins to form a ball.

2. Shape dough into 1½-inch balls; roll in additional sugar. Place about 2 inches apart on ungreased baking sheets; flatten.

3. Bake cookies 17 to 19 minutes or just until set and edges are lightly browned. Remove cookies from baking sheets to wire rack to cool.

Makes 2 to 2½ dozen cookies

Holiday Red Raspberry Chocolate Bars

2½ **cups all-purpose flour**
1 **cup sugar**
¾ **cup finely chopped pecans**
1 **cup (2 sticks) cold butter or margarine**
1 **egg, beaten**
1 **jar (12 ounces) seedless red raspberry jam**
1⅔ **cups HERSHEY'S Milk Chocolate Chips, HERSHEY'S Semi-Sweet Chocolate Chips, HERSHEY'S Raspberry Chips, or HERSHEY'S MINI KISSES™ Milk Chocolates**

1. Heat oven to 350°F. Grease 13×9×2-inch baking pan.

2. Stir together flour, sugar, pecans, butter and egg in large bowl. Cut in butter with pastry blender or fork until mixture resembles coarse crumbs; set aside 1½ cups crumb mixture. Press remaining crumb mixture on bottom of prepared pan; spread jam over top. Sprinkle with chocolate chips. Crumble remaining crumb mixture evenly over top.

3. Bake 40 to 45 minutes or until lightly browned. Cool completely in pan on wire rack; cut into bars.

Makes 36 bars

Chocolate Nut Bars

½ **cup uncooked quick oats**
½ **cup hazelnuts, chopped**
½ **cup walnuts, chopped**
¾ **cup powdered sugar**
8 **ounces (1¼ cups) semisweet chocolate chips**
1 **tablespoon shortening**
2 **tablespoons butter**
½ **teaspoon salt**
⅓ **cup corn syrup**
½ **teaspoon vanilla**

1. Preheat oven to 350°F. Line 8-inch square baking pan with foil, pressing foil into corners to cover completely and leaving 1-inch overhang on sides.

2. Spread oats on ungreased baking sheet. Bake 8 to 10 minutes or until light golden brown. Let cool; place in large bowl. *Reduce oven temperature to 325°F.* Spread hazelnuts and walnuts on baking sheet. Bake 9 to 11 minutes or just until cut sides begin to brown lightly. Let cool; add to toasted oats. Stir in powdered sugar; set aside.

3. Heat chocolate chips and shortening in small heavy saucepan over very low heat, stirring constantly, until melted and smooth. Remove from heat. Spread evenly on bottom of prepared 8-inch square pan. Let stand in cool place 15 to 20 minutes or until chocolate mixture begins to set, but is not firm.

4. Combine butter and salt in microwavable bowl. Microwave at HIGH 20 to 30 seconds or until butter is melted and foamy. Stir in corn syrup; let cool slightly and add vanilla. Stir corn syrup mixture into oat mixture just until moistened. Gently spoon over chocolate, spreading evenly into corners. Score lightly into 4 strips, then score each strip into 6 pieces. Cover tightly with plastic wrap and refrigerate at least 4 hours or until firm.

5. Remove bars from pan, lifting foil by edges. Place on cutting board; cut along score lines into 24 pieces. Remove foil. Store in airtight container in refrigerator.

Makes 24 bars

> *Hazelnuts have bitter brown skins that should be removed. Heat the nuts in a 350°F oven for 10 to 15 minutes until the skins begin to flake. Then rub the nuts vigorously inside a dishtowel until most of skins come off.*

Chocolate Nut Bars

Rum Fruitcake Cookies

1 cup sugar
¾ cup shortening
3 eggs
⅓ cup orange juice
1 tablespoon rum extract
3 cups all-purpose flour
2 teaspoons baking powder
1 teaspoon baking soda
1 teaspoon salt
2 cups (8 ounces) chopped candied mixed fruit
1 cup raisins
1 cup nuts, coarsely chopped

1. Preheat oven to 375°F. Lightly grease cookie sheets; set aside. Beat sugar and shortening in large bowl until fluffy. Add eggs, orange juice and rum extract; beat 2 minutes.

2. Combine flour, baking powder, baking soda and salt in small bowl. Add candied fruit, raisins and nuts. Stir into creamed mixture. Drop dough by rounded teaspoonfuls 2 inches apart onto prepared cookie sheets. Bake 10 to 12 minutes or until golden. Let cookies stand on cookie sheets 2 minutes. Remove to wire racks; cool completely.   *Makes about 6 dozen cookies*

Holiday Mini Kisses Treasure Cookies

1½ cups graham cracker crumbs
½ cup all-purpose flour
2 teaspoons baking powder
1 can (14 ounces) sweetened condensed milk (not evaporated milk)
½ cup (1 stick) butter, softened
1⅓ cups MOUNDS® Coconut Flakes
1 cup HERSHEY'S MINI KISSES™ Milk Chocolates or Semi-Sweet Chocolates
1⅓ cups (10-ounce package) HERSHEY'S Holiday Bits

1. Heat oven to 375°F. Stir together graham cracker crumbs, flour and baking powder in small bowl; set aside.

2. Beat sweetened condensed milk and butter until smooth; add reserved crumb mixture, mixing well. Stir in coconut, Mini Kisses™ and Holiday Bits. Drop by rounded tablespoons onto ungreased cookie sheet.

3. Bake 8 to 10 minutes or until lightly browned. Cool 1 minute; remove from cookie sheet to wire rack. Cool completely.   *Makes about 3 dozen cookies*

Variation: Use 1¾ cups (10-ounce package) HERSHEY'S MINI KISSES™ Milk Chocolate or Semi-Sweet Baking Pieces and 1 cup coarsely chopped walnuts. Omit Holiday Bits. Proceed as directed above.

Almond-Orange Shortbread

1 cup (4 ounces) sliced almonds, divided
2 cups all-purpose flour
1 cup cold butter, cut into pieces
½ cup sugar
½ cup cornstarch
2 tablespoons grated orange peel
1 teaspoon almond extract

1. Preheat oven to 350°F. To toast almonds, spread ¾ cup almonds in single layer in large baking pan. Bake 6 minutes or until golden brown, stirring frequently. Remove almonds from oven. Cool completely in pan. *Reduce oven temperature to 325°F.*

2. Place toasted almonds in food processor. Process using on/off pulses until almonds are coarsely chopped.

3. Add flour, butter, sugar, cornstarch, orange peel and almond extract to food processor. Process using on/off pulses until mixture resembles coarse crumbs.

4. Press dough firmly and evenly into 10×8½-inch rectangle on large ungreased cookie sheet with fingers. Score dough into 1¼-inch squares with knife. Press one slice of remaining almonds in center of each square.

5. Bake 30 to 40 minutes or until shortbread is firm when pressed and lightly browned.

6. Immediately cut into squares along score lines with sharp knife. Remove cookies with spatula to wire racks; cool completely.

7. Store loosely covered at room temperature up to 1 week.

Makes about 5 dozen cookies

Double Chocolate Fantasy Bars

2 cups chocolate cookie crumbs
⅓ cup (5⅓ tablespoons) butter or margarine, melted
1 (14-ounce) can sweetened condensed milk
1¾ cups "M&M's"® Semi-Sweet Chocolate Mini Baking Bits
1 cup shredded coconut
1 cup chopped walnuts or pecans

Preheat oven to 350°F. In large bowl combine cookie crumbs and butter; press mixture onto bottom of 13×9×2-inch baking pan. Pour condensed milk evenly over crumbs. Combine "M&M's"® Semi-Sweet Chocolate Mini Baking Bits, coconut and nuts. Sprinkle mixture evenly over condensed milk; press down lightly. Bake 25 to 30 minutes or until set. Cool completely. Cut into bars. Store in tightly covered container.

Makes 32 bars

Buttery Almond Cutouts

1½ cups granulated sugar
1 cup butter, softened
¾ cup sour cream
2 eggs
3 teaspoons almond extract, divided
1 teaspoon vanilla
4⅓ cups all-purpose flour
1 teaspoon baking powder
1 teaspoon baking soda
½ teaspoon salt
2 cups powdered sugar
2 tablespoons milk
1 tablespoon light corn syrup
Assorted food colorings

1. Beat granulated sugar and butter in large bowl until light and fluffy. Add sour cream, eggs, 2 teaspoons almond extract and vanilla; beat until smooth. Add flour, baking powder, baking soda and salt; beat just until well blended.

2. Divide dough into 4 pieces; flatten each piece into a disc. Wrap each disc tightly with plastic wrap. Refrigerate at least 3 hours or up to 3 days.

3. Combine powdered sugar, milk, corn syrup and remaining 1 teaspoon almond extract in small bowl; stir until smooth. Cover and refrigerate up to 3 days.

4. Preheat oven to 375°F. Working with 1 disc of dough at a time, roll out on floured surface to ¼-inch thickness. Cut dough into desired shapes using 2½-inch cookie cutters. Place about 2 inches apart on ungreased baking sheets. Bake 7 to 8 minutes or until edges are firm and bottoms are brown. Remove from baking sheets to wire racks to cool.

5. Separate powdered sugar mixture into 3 or 4 batches in small bowls; tint each batch with desired food coloring. Frost cookies.   *Makes about 3 dozen cookies*

Note: To freeze dough, place wrapped discs in resealable plastic food storage bags. Thaw at room temperature before using. Or, cut out dough, bake and cool cookies completely. Freeze unglazed cookies for up to 2 months. Thaw and glaze as desired.

Pumpkin White Chocolate Drops

2 cups butter, softened
2 cups granulated sugar
1 can (16 ounces) solid pack pumpkin
2 eggs
4 cups all-purpose flour
2 teaspoons pumpkin pie spice
1 teaspoon baking powder
½ teaspoon baking soda
1 bag (12 ounces) white chocolate chips
1 container (16 ounces) cream cheese frosting
¼ cup packed brown sugar

1. Preheat oven to 375°F. Grease cookie sheets.

2. Beat butter and granulated sugar in large bowl until light and fluffy. Add pumpkin and eggs; beat until smooth. Add flour, pumpkin pie spice, baking powder and baking soda; beat just until well blended. Stir in white chocolate chips.

3. Drop dough by teaspoonfuls about 2 inches apart onto prepared cookie sheets. Bake about 16 minutes or until set and bottoms are brown. Cool 1 minute on cookie sheets. Remove to wire racks; cool.

4. Combine frosting and brown sugar in small bowl. Spread on warm cookies.

Makes about 6 dozen cookies

Sensational Peppermint Pattie Brownies

24 small (1½-inch) YORK® Peppermint Patties
1½ cups (3 sticks) butter or margarine, melted
3 cups sugar
1 tablespoon vanilla extract
5 eggs
2 cups all-purpose flour
1 cup HERSHEY₅S Cocoa
1 teaspoon baking powder
1 teaspoon salt

1. Heat oven to 350°F. Remove wrappers from peppermint patties. Grease 13×9×2-inch baking pan.

2. Stir together butter, sugar and vanilla in large bowl. Add eggs; beat until well blended. Stir together flour, cocoa, baking powder and salt; gradually add to butter mixture, blending well. Reserve 2 cups batter. Spread remaining batter into prepared pan. Arrange peppermint patties about ½ inch apart in single layer over batter. Spread reserved batter over patties.

3. Bake 50 to 55 minutes or until brownies pull away from sides of pan. Cool completely in pan on wire rack.

Makes about 36 brownies

Crispy Thumbprint Cookies

1 package (18.25 ounces) yellow cake mix
½ cup vegetable oil
¼ cup water
1 egg
3 cups crisp rice cereal, crushed
½ cup chopped walnuts
6 tablespoons raspberry or strawberry preserves

1. Preheat oven to 375°F.

2. Combine cake mix, oil, water and egg. Beat at medium speed of electric mixer until well blended. Add cereal and walnuts; mix until well blended.

3. Drop by heaping teaspoonfuls about 2 inches apart onto ungreased baking sheets. Use thumb to make indentation in each cookie. Spoon about ½ teaspoon preserves into center of each cookie.

4. Bake 9 to 11 minutes or until golden brown. Cool cookies 1 minute on baking sheet; remove from baking sheet to wire rack to cool completely.

Makes 3 dozen cookies

Festive Lebkuchen

3 tablespoons butter
1 cup packed brown sugar
¼ cup honey
1 egg
Grated peel and juice of 1 lemon
3 cups all-purpose flour
2 teaspoons ground allspice
½ teaspoon baking soda
½ teaspoon salt
White decorator's frosting

Melt butter with brown sugar and honey in medium saucepan over low heat, stirring constantly. Pour into large bowl. Cool 30 minutes. Add egg, lemon peel and juice; beat 2 minutes with electric mixer at high speed. Stir in flour, allspice, baking soda and salt until well blended. Cover; refrigerate overnight or up to 3 days.

Preheat oven to 350°F. Grease cookie sheets. Roll out dough to ½-inch thickness on lightly floured surface with lightly floured rolling pin. Cut out with 3-inch cookie cutters. Transfer to prepared cookie sheets. Bake 15 to 18 minutes until edges are light brown. Cool 1 minute. Remove to wire racks; cool completely. Decorate with white frosting. Store in airtight container.

Makes 1 dozen cookies

Crispy Thumbprint Cookies

Mexican Chocolate Macaroons

1 package (8 ounces) semisweet baking chocolate, divided
1¾ cups plus ⅓ cup whole almonds, divided
¾ cup sugar
1 teaspoon ground cinnamon
1 teaspoon vanilla
2 egg whites

1. Preheat oven to 400°F. Grease baking sheets. Place 5 squares chocolate in food processor; process until coarsely chopped. Add 1¾ cups almonds and sugar; process using on/off pulses until mixture is finely ground. Add cinnamon, vanilla and egg whites; process just until mixture forms moist dough.

2. Form dough into 1-inch balls (dough will be sticky). Place about 2 inches apart on prepared baking sheets. Press 1 almond on top of each cookie.

3. Bake 8 to 10 minutes or just until set. Cool 2 minutes on baking sheets. Remove cookies from baking sheets to wire racks. Cool completely.

4. Heat remaining 3 squares chocolate in small saucepan over very low heat until melted. Spoon chocolate into small resealable plastic food storage bag. Cut small corner off bottom of bag; drizzle chocolate over cookies.   *Makes 3 dozen cookies*

Tip: For longer storage, allow cookies to stand until chocolate drizzle is set. Store in airtight containers.

Cinnamony Apple Streusel Bars

1¼ cups graham cracker crumbs
1¼ cups all-purpose flour
¾ cup packed brown sugar, divided
¼ cup granulated sugar
1 teaspoon ground cinnamon
¾ cup butter, melted
2 cups chopped apples (2 medium apples, cored and peeled)
Glaze (recipe follows)

Preheat oven to 350°F. Grease 13×9-inch baking pan. Combine graham cracker crumbs, flour, ½ cup brown sugar, granulated sugar, cinnamon and melted butter in large bowl until well blended; reserve 1 cup. Press remaining crumb mixture into bottom of prepared pan. Bake 8 minutes. Remove from oven; set aside.

Toss remaining ¼ cup brown sugar with apples in medium bowl until dissolved; arrange apples over baked crust. Sprinkle reserved 1 cup crumb mixture over filling. Bake 30 to 35 minutes or until apples are tender. Remove pan to wire rack; cool completely. Drizzle with Glaze. Cut into bars.   *Makes 3 dozen bars*

Glaze: Combine ½ cup powdered sugar and 1 tablespoon milk in small bowl until well blended.

Chippy Chewy Bars

½ cup (1 stick) butter or margarine
1½ cups graham cracker crumbs
1⅔ cups (10-ounce package) REESE'S® Peanut Butter Chips, divided
1½ cups MOUNDS® Sweetened Coconut Flakes
1 can (14 ounces) sweetened condensed milk (not evaporated milk)
1 cup HERSHEY'S Semi-Sweet Chocolate Chips or HERSHEY'S MINI CHIPS™ Semi-Sweet Chocolate Chips
1½ teaspoons shortening (do *not* use butter, margarine, spread or oil)

1. Heat oven to 350°F.

2. Place butter in 13×9×2-inch baking pan. Heat in oven until melted. Remove pan from oven. Sprinkle graham cracker crumbs evenly over butter; press down with fork. Layer 1 cup peanut butter chips over crumbs; sprinkle coconut over peanut butter chips. Layer remaining ⅔ cup peanut butter chips over coconut; drizzle sweetened condensed milk evenly over top. Press down firmly.

3. Bake 20 minutes or until lightly browned.

4. Place chocolate chips and shortening in small microwave-safe bowl. Microwave at HIGH (100%) 1 minute; stir. If necessary, microwave at HIGH an additional 15 seconds at a time, stirring after each heating, just until chips are melted when stirred. Drizzle evenly over top of baked mixture. Cool completely in pan on wire rack. Cut into bars. *Makes about 48 bars*

Note: For lighter drizzle, use ½ cup chocolate chips and ¾ teaspoon shortening. Microwave at HIGH 30 seconds to 1 minute; stir. If necessary, microwave at HIGH an additional 15 seconds at a time, stirring after each heating, just until chips are melted when stirred.

Festive Fudge Blossoms

¼ cup butter, softened
1 box (18.25 ounces) chocolate fudge cake mix
1 egg, lightly beaten
2 tablespoons water
¾ to 1 cup finely chopped walnuts
48 chocolate star candies

1. Preheat oven to 350°F. Cut butter into cake mix in large bowl until mixture resembles coarse crumbs. Stir in egg and water until well blended.

2. Shape dough into ½-inch balls; roll in walnuts, pressing nuts gently into dough. Place about 2 inches apart on ungreased baking sheets.

3. Bake cookies 12 minutes or until puffed and nearly set. Place chocolate star in center of each cookie; bake 1 minute. Cool 2 minutes on baking sheets. Transfer cookies to wire racks to cool completely. *Makes 4 dozen cookies*

Choco-Coco Pecan Crisps

½ cup butter, softened
1 cup packed light brown sugar
1 egg
1 teaspoon vanilla
1½ cups all-purpose flour
1 cup chopped pecans
⅓ cup unsweetened cocoa powder
½ teaspoon baking soda
1 cup flaked coconut

Cream butter and brown sugar in large bowl until light and fluffy. Beat in egg and vanilla. Combine flour, pecans, cocoa and baking soda in small bowl until well blended. Add to creamed mixture, blending until stiff dough is formed. Sprinkle coconut on work surface. Divide dough into 4 parts. Shape each part into a roll about 1½ inches in diameter; roll in coconut until thickly coated. Wrap in plastic wrap; refrigerate until firm, at least 1 hour or up to 2 weeks. (For longer storage, freeze up to 6 weeks.)

Preheat oven to 350°F. Cut rolls into ⅛-inch-thick slices. Place 2 inches apart on ungreased cookie sheets. Bake 10 to 13 minutes or until firm, but not overly browned. Remove to wire racks to cool. *Makes about 6 dozen cookies*

Coconut Pecan Bars

¾ cup (1½ sticks) butter or margarine, softened, divided
1¼ cups granulated sugar, divided
½ cup plus 3 tablespoons all-purpose flour, divided
1½ cups finely chopped pecans, divided
2 large eggs
1 tablespoon vanilla extract
1¾ cups "M&M's"® Chocolate Mini Baking Bits, divided
1 cup shredded coconut

Preheat oven to 350°F. Lightly grease 13×9×2-inch baking pan; set aside. Melt ¼ cup butter. In large bowl combine ¾ cup sugar, ½ cup flour and ½ cup nuts; add melted butter and mix well. Press mixture onto bottom of prepared pan. Bake 10 minutes or until set; cool slightly. In large bowl cream remaining ½ cup butter and ½ cup sugar; beat in eggs and vanilla. Combine 1 cup "M&M's"® Chocolate Mini Baking Bits and remaining 3 tablespoons flour; stir into creamed mixture. Spread mixture over cooled crust. Combine coconut and remaining 1 cup nuts; sprinkle over batter. Sprinkle remaining ¾ cup "M&M's"® Chocolate Mini Baking Bits over coconut and nuts; pat down lightly. Bake 25 to 30 minutes or until set. Cool completely. Cut into bars. Store in tightly covered container. *Makes 24 bars*

VISIONS OF SUGARPLUMS

Holiday Peppermint Bark

2 cups (12-ounce package) NESTLÉ® TOLL HOUSE® Premier White Morsels
24 hard peppermint candies, unwrapped

LINE baking sheet with wax paper.

MICROWAVE morsels in medium, microwave-safe bowl on MEDIUM-HIGH (70%) power for 1 minute; stir. Microwave at additional 10- to 20-second intervals, stirring until smooth.

PLACE peppermint candies in *heavy-duty* resealable plastic food storage bag. Crush candies using rolling pin or other heavy object. While holding strainer over melted morsels, pour crushed candy into strainer. Shake to release all small candy pieces; reserve larger candy pieces. Stir morsel-peppermint mixture.

SPREAD mixture to desired thickness on prepared baking sheet. Sprinkle with reserved candy pieces; press in lightly. Let stand for about 1 hour or until firm. Break into pieces. Store in airtight container at room temperature.   *Makes about 1 pound candy*

Peanut Butter Fudge

1 cup creamy peanut butter
1 cup sweetened condensed milk
1 cup powdered sugar
1 teaspoon vanilla
½ cup raisins, chopped

1. Butter 8-inch square pan.

2. Combine peanut butter, condensed milk, powdered sugar and vanilla in medium bowl. Beat with electric mixer until smooth. Stir in raisins. Press into prepared pan. Score fudge into squares with knife. Refrigerate until firm.

3. Cut into squares. Store in refrigerator.   *Makes about 1½ pounds*

Holiday Peppermint Bark

Black Russian Truffles

8 ounces premium bittersweet chocolate, broken into 2-inch pieces
¼ cup whipping cream
2 tablespoons butter
3½ tablespoons coffee-flavored liqueur
1½ tablespoons vodka
1 cup chopped toasted walnuts

1. Place chocolate in food processor; process until chocolate is chopped.

2. Combine cream and butter in 1-cup glass measuring cup. Microwave at HIGH 1½ minutes or until butter is melted and cream begins to boil.

3. With food processor running, pour hot cream mixture through food tube; process until chocolate melts. Add liqueur and vodka; process until blended. Pour chocolate mixture into medium bowl; cover with plastic wrap and refrigerate overnight.

4. Shape chocolate mixture into 1-inch balls. Roll in walnuts. Store in airtight container in refrigerator. Let stand at room temperature 2 to 3 hours before serving.

Makes about 2½ dozen truffles

Brandy Truffles: Add 3½ tablespoons brandy to chocolate mixture in Step 3 in place of coffee-flavored liqueur and vodka. Roll truffles in 1 cup powdered sugar in place of walnuts.

Hazelnut Truffles: Add 3½ tablespoons hazelnut-flavored liqueur and 1½ tablespoons gold tequila to chocolate mixture in Step 3 in place of coffee-flavored liqueur and vodka. Roll truffles in 1 cup chopped toasted hazelnuts in place of walnuts.

Toasted Almond Bark

½ cup slivered almonds
12 ounces white chocolate, coarsely chopped
1 tablespoon shortening

1. Preheat oven to 325°F. Spread almonds on baking sheet. Bake 12 minutes or until golden brown, stirring occasionally.

3. Meanwhile, butter another baking sheet. Spread warm almonds on buttered baking sheet.

4. Melt white chocolate with shortening in heavy, small saucepan over very low heat, stirring constantly.

5. Spoon evenly over almonds, spreading about ¼ inch thick. Refrigerate until almost firm. Cut into squares, but do not remove from baking sheet. Refrigerate until firm.

Makes about 1 pound

Creamy Double Decker Fudge

1 cup REESE'S® Peanut Butter Chips
1 can (14 ounces) sweetened condensed milk (not evaporated milk), divided
1 teaspoon vanilla extract, divided
1 cup HERSHEY'S Semi-Sweet Chocolate Chips

1. Line 8-inch square pan with foil. Place peanut butter chips and ⅔ cup sweetened condensed milk in small microwave-safe bowl. Microwave at HIGH (100%) 1 to 1½ minutes, stirring after 1 minute, until chips are melted and mixture is smooth when stirred. Stir in ½ teaspoon vanilla; spread evenly into prepared pan.

2. Place remaining sweetened condensed milk and chocolate chips in another small microwave-safe bowl; repeat above microwave procedure. Stir in remaining ½ teaspoon vanilla; spread evenly over peanut butter layer.

3. Cover; refrigerate until firm. Remove from pan; place on cutting board. Peel off foil. Cut into squares. Store tightly covered in refrigerator.

Makes about 4 dozen pieces or 1½ pounds

Note: For best results, do not double this recipe.

Prep Time: 15 minutes
Cook Time: 3 minutes
Chill Time: 2 hours

Merri-Mint Truffles

1 package (10 ounces) mint chocolate chips
⅓ cup whipping cream
¼ cup butter or margarine
1 container (3½ ounces) chocolate sprinkles

Melt chocolate chips with cream and butter in heavy medium saucepan over low heat, stirring occasionally. Pour into pie pan. Refrigerate about 2 hours or until mixture is fudgy, but soft.

Shape about 1 tablespoonful of mixture into 1¼-inch ball. Repeat with remaining mixture. Roll balls in your palms to form uniform round shapes; place on waxed paper.

Place sprinkles in shallow bowl. Roll balls in sprinkles; place in miniature paper candy cups. (If coating mixture won't stick because truffle has set, roll between your palms until outside is soft.) Store in airtight container up to 3 days in refrigerator or several weeks in freezer.

Makes about 24 truffles

Hawaiian Toffee

1 jar (3½ ounces) macadamia nuts (¾ cup), coarsely chopped
1 cup unsalted butter
1 cup sugar
2 tablespoons water
¼ teaspoon salt
1 teaspoon vanilla
4 ounces milk chocolate chips
1 cup flaked coconut, toasted

1. Line 9-inch square pan with foil, extending edges over sides of pan. Sprinkle nuts evenly in single layer in prepared pan.

2. Combine butter, sugar, water and salt in medium saucepan. Bring to a boil over medium heat, stirring frequently. Attach candy thermometer to side of pan. Continue boiling about 20 minutes or until sugar mixture reaches hard-crack stage (305° to 310°F) on candy thermometer, stirring frequently. Remove from heat; stir in vanilla. Immediately pour over nuts in pan, spreading to edges with spatula. Cool completely.

3. Place chocolate in small microwave-safe bowl. Microwave at MEDIUM (50% power) 4 to 5 minutes until chocolate is melted, stirring every 2 minutes.

4. Lift toffee out of pan using foil; spread chocolate evenly over toffee. Sprinkle with toasted coconut. Refrigerate about 30 minutes or until chocolate is set. Bring to room temperature before breaking toffee. Break toffee into pieces. Store in airtight container at room temperature between sheets of waxed paper.

Makes about 1¼ pounds toffee

Stuffed Pecans

½ cup semisweet chocolate chips
¼ cup sweetened condensed milk
½ teaspoon vanilla
Powdered sugar (about ½ cup)
80 large pecan halves

Melt chips in small saucepan over very low heat, stirring constantly. Remove from heat. Stir in sweetened condensed milk and vanilla until smooth. Stir in enough sugar to make stiff mixture. Refrigerate, if needed.

Place 1 rounded teaspoonful chocolate mixture on flat side of 1 pecan half. Top with another pecan half. Repeat with remaining pecans and chocolate mixture. Store in refrigerator.

Makes about 40 candies

Hawaiian Toffee

Chocolate Mint Truffles

1¾ cups (11.5-ounce package) NESTLÉ® TOLL HOUSE® Milk Chocolate Morsels
1 cup (6 ounces) NESTLÉ® TOLL HOUSE® Semi-Sweet Chocolate Morsels
¾ cup heavy whipping cream
1 tablespoon peppermint extract
1½ cups finely chopped walnuts, toasted, or NESTLÉ® TOLL HOUSE®
  Baking Cocoa

LINE baking sheet with wax paper.

PLACE milk chocolate and semi-sweet morsels in large mixer bowl. Heat cream to a gentle boil in small saucepan; pour over morsels. Let stand for 1 minute; stir until smooth. Stir in peppermint extract. Cover with plastic wrap; refrigerate for 35 to 45 minutes or until slightly thickened. Stir just until color lightens slightly. (*Do not overmix or truffles will be grainy.*)

DROP by rounded teaspoonful onto prepared baking sheet; refrigerate for 10 to 15 minutes. Shape into balls; roll in walnuts or cocoa. Store in airtight container in refrigerator.   *Makes about 48 truffles*

Variation: After rolling chocolate mixture into balls, freeze for 30 to 40 minutes. Microwave 1¾ cups (11.5-ounce package) NESTLÉ® TOLL HOUSE® Milk Chocolate Morsels and 3 tablespoons vegetable shortening in medium, microwave-safe bowl on MEDIUM-HIGH (70%) power for 1 minute; stir. Microwave at additional 10- to 20-second intervals, stirring until smooth. Dip truffles into chocolate mixture; shake off excess. Place on foil-lined baking sheets. Refrigerate for 15 to 20 minutes or until set. Store in airtight container in refrigerator.

Marshmallow Cups

2 cups (11½ ounces) milk chocolate chips
2 tablespoons shortening
1 cup (½ of 7-ounce jar) marshmallow creme

1. Line 18 mini-muffin cups with double-thickness paper cups or foil cups.

2. Melt chips with shortening in heavy, small saucepan over very low heat, stirring constantly.

3. Spoon about ½ tablespoonful chocolate mixture into each cup. With back of spoon, bring chocolate up side of each cup; let set.

4. Spoon 1 tablespoonful marshmallow creme into each chocolate cup, using spoons dipped in hot water. Spread with small spatula.

5. Spoon about ½ tablespoonful of remaining chocolate over each marshmallow cup. Refrigerate until firm.   *Makes 18 cups*

Easy Turtle Fudge

1 package (12 ounces) semisweet chocolate chips (2 cups)
2 ounces bittersweet or semisweet chocolate, chopped
1 cup sweetened condensed milk
¼ teaspoon salt
30 caramel candies, unwrapped
1 tablespoon water
40 pecan halves

1. Grease 11×7-inch pan. Melt chips in heavy, medium saucepan over very low heat, stirring constantly. Remove from heat. Stir in bittersweet chocolate until melted. Stir in sweetened condensed milk and salt until smooth.

2. Spread evenly in prepared pan; cover with foil. Refrigerate until firm.

3. Cut fudge into squares. Transfer to baking sheet lined with waxed paper.

4. Place caramels and water in heavy small saucepan. Heat over low heat until melted, stirring frequently. Drizzle or top fudge pieces with caramel mixture. Top each piece with 1 pecan half. Store in airtight container in freezer. Bring to room temperature before serving. *Makes 40 candies*

Butterscotch Rocky Road

1½ cups miniature marshmallows
1 cup coarsely chopped pecans
2 cups (12 ounces) butterscotch chips
½ cup sweetened condensed milk

1. Butter 13×9-inch pan. Spread marshmallows and pecans evenly on bottom of pan.

2. Melt butterscotch chips in heavy, medium saucepan over low heat, stirring constantly. Stir in condensed milk.

3. Pour butterscotch mixture over marshmallows and pecans, covering entire mixture. If necessary, use knife or small spatula to help cover marshmallows and nuts with butterscotch mixture. Let stand in pan until set.

4. Cut into squares. Store in refrigerator. *Makes about 1 pound*

Easy Turtle Fudge

White Christmas Jewel Fudge

3 (6-ounce) packages premium white chocolate chips
1 (14-ounce) can EAGLE® BRAND Sweetened Condensed Milk (NOT evaporated milk)
1½ teaspoons vanilla extract
⅛ teaspoon salt
½ cup chopped green candied cherries, if desired
½ cup chopped red candied cherries, if desired

1. In heavy saucepan over low heat, melt chips with Eagle Brand, vanilla and salt. Remove from heat; stir in cherries, if desired. Spread evenly in foil-lined 8- or 9-inch square pan. Chill 2 hours or until firm.

2. Turn fudge onto cutting board; peel off foil and cut into squares. Store covered in refrigerator.

Makes 2¼ pounds fudge

Eggnog Truffles

2 cups (11½ ounces) milk chocolate chips
2 tablespoons butter or margarine
½ cup eggnog
36 chocolate cups, either purchased or homemade (recipe follows)

1. Heat chocolate chips, butter and eggnog in heavy, medium saucepan over low heat, stirring occasionally until melted. Pour into pie pan. Refrigerate until mixture is thick but soft, about 2 hours.

2. Spoon truffle mixture into pastry bag fitted with large star tip. Pipe mixture into chocolate cups.

3. Truffles can be refrigerated 2 to 3 days or frozen several weeks.

Makes about 36 truffles

Chocolate Cups

2 cups (12 ounces) semisweet chocolate chips
1 tablespoon shortening

1. Melt chips with shortening in heavy, small saucepan over very low heat, stirring constantly.

2. Spoon about ½ tablespoonful chocolate mixture into each of about 36 small foil candy cups. With back of spoon, bring some of chocolate up side of each cup, coating foil completely. Let stand in cool place or refrigerate until firm.

Makes about 36 cups

Hint: To remove foil cups, cut slit in bottom of cup and peel foil up from bottom. Do not peel down from top edge.

White Christmas Jewel Fudge

Coconut Balls

½ cup golden raisins, chopped
½ cup pitted prunes or dates, chopped
½ cup graham cracker crumbs
½ cup powdered sugar
1 tablespoon grated orange peel
½ cup sweetened condensed milk
1 cup shredded coconut

1. Combine raisins, prunes, graham cracker crumbs, sugar and orange peel in medium bowl. Stir in condensed milk. Refrigerate until firm enough to shape into balls, about 30 minutes.

2. Place coconut in shallow bowl.

3. For each candy, shape scant 1 tablespoonful of mixture into 1-inch ball. Roll in coconut. Store in refrigerator.

Makes 30 candies

Buttermilk Fudge

1 cup buttermilk
1 teaspoon baking soda
2 tablespoons corn syrup
2 tablespoons butter or margarine
2 cups sugar
1 teaspoon vanilla
1 cup chopped pecans

1. Butter 8-inch square pan. Lightly butter side of 3-quart saucepan. Combine buttermilk and baking soda in prepared saucepan, then add corn syrup, butter and sugar. Cook over medium heat, stirring constantly, until sugar dissolves and mixture comes to a boil. Wash down side of pan with pastry brush frequently dipped in hot water to remove sugar crystals.

2. Reduce heat to low. Carefully clip candy thermometer to side of pan (do not let bulb touch bottom of pan). Stir mixture occasionally. Continue to cook until mixture reaches soft-ball stage (238°F).

3. Pour into large heatproof mixer bowl. Cool to lukewarm (about 110°F). Add vanilla and beat with heavy-duty electric mixer until thick. Beat in pecans when candy starts to lose its gloss. Spread in prepared pan. Score fudge into squares with knife. Refrigerate until firm. Cut into squares. Store in refrigerator.

Makes about 1 pound

Note: Mixture boils up! Make sure to use a large (3-quart) saucepan.

Coconut Balls

Cashew Macadamia Crunch

2 cups (11.5 ounce package) HERSHEY'S Milk Chocolate Chips
¾ cup coarsely chopped salted or unsalted cashews
¾ cup coarsely chopped salted or unsalted macadamia nuts
½ cup (1 stick) butter, softened
½ cup sugar
2 tablespoons light corn syrup

1. Line 9-inch square pan with foil, extending foil over edges of pan. Butter foil. Cover bottom of prepared pan with chocolate chips.

2. Combine cashews, macadamia nuts, butter, sugar and corn syrup in large heavy skillet; cook over low heat, stirring constantly, until butter is melted and sugar is dissolved. Increase heat to medium; cook, stirring constantly, until mixture begins to cling together and turns golden brown.

3. Pour mixture over chocolate chips in pan, spreading evenly. Cool. Refrigerate until chocolate is firm. Remove from pan; peel off foil. Break into pieces. Store tightly covered in cool, dry place. *Makes about 1½ pounds*

Prep Time: 30 minutes
Cook Time: 10 minutes
Cool Time: 40 minutes
Chill Time: 3 hours

Chocolate-Nut Squares

1 cup (6 ounces) semisweet chocolate chips
1 cup milk chocolate chips
1 tablespoon shortening
1 package (14 ounces) caramels
2 tablespoons butter or margarine
3 tablespoons milk
2 cups coarsely chopped pecans

Line 8-inch square pan with buttered foil; set aside. Melt both kinds of chips with shortening in heavy, small saucepan over very low heat, stirring constantly. Spoon half the chocolate mixture into prepared pan, spreading evenly over bottom and ¼ inch up sides of pan. Refrigerate until firm.

Meanwhile, combine caramels, butter and milk in heavy, medium saucepan. Cook over medium heat, stirring constantly. When mixture is smooth, stir in pecans. Cool to lukewarm. Spread caramel mixture evenly over chocolate in pan. Melt remaining chocolate mixture again over very low heat, stirring constantly; spread over caramel layer. Refrigerate until almost firm. Cut into squares. Store in refrigerator.

Makes about 2 pounds

Tip: Squares are easier to cut without breaking if chocolate is not completely firm.

Chocolate Chip Cookie Dough Fudge

⅓ **cup butter, melted**
⅓ **cup packed brown sugar**
¾ **cup all-purpose flour**
½ **teaspoon salt, divided**
1⅓ **cups mini semisweet chocolate chips, divided**
1 **package (1 pound) powdered sugar (about 4 cups)**
1 **package (8 ounces) cream cheese, softened**
1 **teaspoon vanilla**

1. Line 8- or 9-inch square pan with foil, leaving 1-inch overhang on sides. Lightly butter foil.

2. Combine butter and brown sugar in small bowl. Stir in flour and ¼ teaspoon salt. Stir in ⅓ cup chips.

3. Form dough into a ball. Place on plastic wrap; flatten into a disc. Wrap disc in plastic wrap; freeze 10 minutes or until firm.

4. Unwrap dough and cut into ½-inch pieces; refrigerate.

5. Place powdered sugar, cream cheese, vanilla and remaining ¼ teaspoon salt in large bowl. Beat with electric mixer at low speed until combined. Scrape down side of bowl; beat at medium speed until smooth.

6. Melt remaining 1 cup chips in heavy small saucepan over very low heat, stirring constantly. Remove from heat as soon as chocolate is melted.

7. Add melted chocolate to cream cheese mixture; beat just until blended. Stir in chilled cookie dough pieces.

8. Spread evenly in prepared pan. Score into squares, about 1¼×1¼ inches, while fudge is still warm.

9. Refrigerate until firm. Remove from pan by lifting fudge and foil using foil handles. Place on cutting board; cut along score lines into squares. Remove foil. Store in airtight container in refrigerator. *Makes about 3 to 4 dozen candies*

White Chocolate-Dipped Apricots

3 **ounces white chocolate, coarsely chopped**
20 **dried apricot halves**

Line baking sheet with waxed paper; set aside. Melt white chocolate in bowl over hot (not boiling) water, stirring constantly.

Dip half of each apricot piece in chocolate, coating both sides. Place on prepared baking sheet. Refrigerate until firm. Store in refrigerator in container between layers of waxed paper. *Makes 20 apricots*

Chocolate Truffles

3 cups (18 ounces) semi-sweet chocolate chips
1 (14-ounce) can EAGLE® BRAND Sweetened Condensed Milk (NOT evaporated milk)
1 tablespoon vanilla extract
Coatings: finely chopped toasted nuts, flaked coconut, chocolate sprinkles, colored sugar, unsweetened cocoa, powdered sugar or colored sprinkles

1. In heavy saucepan over low heat, melt chips with Eagle Brand. Remove from heat; stir in vanilla.

2. Chill 2 hours or until firm. Shape into 1-inch balls; roll in desired coating.

3. Chill 1 hour or until firm. Store covered at room temperature.

Makes about 6 dozen truffles

Microwave Directions: In 1-quart glass measure, combine chips and Eagle Brand. Microwave at HIGH (100% power) 3 minutes, stirring after 1½ minutes. Stir until smooth. Proceed as directed above.

Amaretto Truffles: Substitute 3 tablespoons amaretto liqueur and ½ teaspoon almond extract for vanilla. Roll in finely chopped toasted almonds.

Orange Truffles: Substitute 3 tablespoons orange-flavored liqueur for vanilla. Roll in finely chopped toasted almonds mixed with finely grated orange peel.

Rum Truffles: Substitute ¼ cup dark rum for vanilla. Roll in flaked coconut.

Bourbon Truffles: Substitute 3 tablespoons bourbon for vanilla. Roll in finely chopped toasted nuts.

Prep Time: 10 minutes
Chill Time: 3 hours

Peanut Butter Confections

1½ cups nonfat dry milk powder
1 cup creamy peanut butter
1 cup honey
1 cup flaked coconut
1 cup graham cracker crumbs or 1 cup flaked coconut

1. Line baking sheet with waxed paper.

2. Combine dry milk powder, peanut butter, honey and 1 cup coconut in medium bowl. Refrigerate until firm enough to shape into balls, about 30 minutes.

3. Shape scant tablespoonfuls of mixture into 1-inch balls.

4. Place crumbs in shallow bowl. Roll balls in crumbs. Place balls on prepared baking sheet. Refrigerate until set. Store in refrigerator in airtight container.

Makes about 48 balls

Festive Fudge

3 cups (1½ packages, 12 ounces each) HERSHEY'S Semi-Sweet Chocolate Chips
1 can (14 ounces) sweetened condensed milk (not evaporated milk)
    Dash salt
½ to 1 cup chopped nuts (optional)
1½ teaspoons vanilla extract

1. Line 8- or 9-inch square pan with wax paper.

2. Melt chocolate chips with sweetened condensed milk and salt in heavy saucepan over low heat. Remove from heat; stir in nuts, if desired, and vanilla. Spread evenly into prepared pan.

3. Refrigerate 2 hours or until firm. Turn fudge onto cutting board; peel off paper and cut into squares. Store covered in refrigerator.   *Makes about 2 pounds*

Chocolate Peanut Butter Chip Glazed Fudge: Proceed as above; stir in ⅔ cup REESE'S® Peanut Butter Chips in place of nuts. Melt 1 cup REESE'S® Peanut Butter Chips with ½ cup whipping cream; stir until thick and smooth. Spread over fudge.

Marbled Truffles

  6 ounces white chocolate, coarsely chopped
½ cup whipping cream, divided
  1 teaspoon vanilla
  1 cup (6 ounces) semisweet chocolate chips
  1 tablespoon butter or margarine
  2 tablespoons orange-flavored liqueur
¾ cup powdered sugar, sifted

1. Melt white chocolate with ¼ cup whipping cream and vanilla in heavy, medium saucepan over low heat, stirring constantly. Pour into 9-inch square pan. Refrigerate.

2. Melt semisweet chocolate chips with butter and remaining ¼ cup whipping cream in heavy, medium saucepan over low heat, stirring constantly. Whisk in liqueur.

3. Pour chocolate mixture over refrigerated white chocolate mixture. Refrigerate until mixture is fudgy but soft, about 1 hour.

4. Shape about 1 tablespoonful mixture into 1¼-inch ball. To shape, roll mixture in your palms. Repeat with remaining mixture; place truffles on waxed paper.

5. Sift powdered sugar into shallow bowl. Roll truffles in powdered sugar; place in miniature paper candy cups. (If coating mixture won't stick because truffle has set, roll between your palms until outside is soft.) Truffles can be refrigerated 2 to 3 days or frozen several weeks.   *Makes about 30 truffles*

Tropical Sugarplums

½ cup white chocolate chips
¼ cup light corn syrup
½ cup chopped dates
¼ cup chopped maraschino cherries, well drained
1 teaspoon vanilla
¼ teaspoon rum extract
1¼ cups crushed gingersnaps
Flaked coconut

1. Combine white chocolate chips and corn syrup in large skillet. Cook and stir over low heat until melted and smooth.

2. Stir in dates, cherries, vanilla and rum extract until well blended. Add gingersnaps, stirring until well blended. (Mixture will be stiff.)

3. Form mixture into ¾-inch balls; roll in coconut. Place in miniature paper candy cups, if desired. Serve immediately or let stand overnight to allow flavors to blend.

Makes about 2 dozen candies

Prep Time: 20 minutes

Peanut Butter Cups

2 cups (12 ounces) semisweet chocolate chips
1 cup (6 ounces) milk chocolate chips
1½ cups powdered sugar
1 cup crunchy or smooth peanut butter
½ cup vanilla wafer crumbs (about 11 wafers)
6 tablespoons butter or margarine, softened

Line 12 (2½-inch) muffin cups with double-thickness paper cups or foil cups.

Melt both chips in heavy, small saucepan over very low heat, stirring constantly. Spoon about 1 tablespoonful chocolate into each cup. With back of spoon, bring chocolate up side of each cup. Refrigerate until firm, about 20 minutes.

Combine sugar, peanut butter, wafer crumbs and butter in medium bowl. Spoon 2 tablespoons peanut butter mixture into each chocolate cup. Spread with small spatula.

Spoon about 1 tablespoon remaining chocolate over each peanut butter cup. Refrigerate until firm.

Makes 12 cups

Note: To remove paper cups, cut slit in bottom of paper and peel paper up from bottom. Do not peel paper down from top edge.

Triple Layer Chocolate Mints

6 ounces semisweet chocolate, chopped
6 ounces white chocolate, chopped
1 teaspoon peppermint extract
6 ounces milk chocolate, chopped

1. Line 8-inch square pan with foil, leaving 1-inch overhang on sides. Place semisweet chocolate in top of double boiler over simmering water. Stir until melted. Remove from heat.

2. Spread melted chocolate onto bottom of prepared pan. Let stand until firm. (If not firm after 45 minutes, refrigerate 10 minutes.)

3. Melt white chocolate in clean double boiler; stir in peppermint extract. Spread over semisweet chocolate layer. Shake pan to spread evenly. Let stand 45 minutes or until set.

4. Melt milk chocolate in same double boiler. Spread over white chocolate layer. Shake pan to spread evenly. Let stand 45 minutes or until set.

5. Cut mints into 16 (2-inch) squares. Remove from pan by lifting mints and foil with foil handles. Place squares on cutting board.

6. Cut each square diagonally into 2 triangles. Cut in half again to make 64 small triangles. Store in airtight container in refrigerator.   *Makes 64 mints*

Creamy Chocolate Dipped Strawberries

1 cup HERSHEY'S Semi-Sweet Chocolate Chips
½ cup HERSHEY'S Premier White Chips
1 tablespoon shortening (do *not* use butter, margarine, spread or oil)
  Fresh strawberries, rinsed and patted dry (about 2 pints)

1. Line tray with wax paper.

2. Place chocolate chips, white chips and shortening in medium microwave-safe bowl. Microwave at HIGH (100%) 1 minute; stir. If necessary, microwave at HIGH an additional 15 seconds at a time, stirring after each heating, just until chips are melted when stirred. Holding top, dip bottom two-thirds of each strawberry into melted mixture; shake gently to remove excess. Place on prepared tray.

3. Refrigerate about 1 hour or until coating is firm. Cover; refrigerate leftover dipped berries. For best results, use within 24 hours.

Makes about 3 dozen dipped berries

Cookies and Cream Cheesecake Bonbons

24 chocolate cream-filled cookies, divided
1 package (8 ounces) cream cheese, softened
1 cup nonfat dry milk powder
1 teaspoon vanilla
1 package (1 pound) powdered sugar (about 4 cups)
Fresh raspberries and raspberry leaves for garnish

1. Coarsely chop 12 cookies; set aside.

2. Place remaining 12 cookies in food processor; process until fine crumbs form. Place crumbs on baking sheet lined with waxed paper; set aside.

3. Beat cream cheese, dry milk powder and vanilla in medium bowl with electric mixer at medium speed until smooth. Beat in powdered sugar, 1 cup at a time, at low speed until mixture is smooth. Stir in reserved chopped cookies. Refrigerate 2 hours or until firm.

4. Shape rounded tablespoonfuls of cream cheese mixture into balls. Roll balls in reserved cookie crumbs. Garnish, if desired. Store in airtight container in refrigerator. *Makes about 3 dozen bonbons*

Chocolate-Granola Bars

3 cups raisin-and-nut granola
½ cup finely chopped dried apricots
½ cup finely chopped dates
12 ounces white chocolate, coarsely chopped
¼ cup half-and-half or evaporated milk

1. Butter 8-inch square pan. Combine granola, apricots and dates in medium heatproof bowl; set aside.

2. Melt white chocolate with half-and-half in heavy, small saucepan over low heat, stirring constantly.

3. Pour chocolate mixture over granola mixture and stir until coated. Press into prepared pan. Refrigerate until firm.

4. Cut into 2×1-inch bars. Store in refrigerator. *Makes 32 bars*

Cookies and Cream Cheesecake Bonbons

Caramel-Nut Chocolate Cups

36 Chocolate Cups (page 162) or purchased chocolate liqueur cups
¾ cup plus 36 pecan halves, divided
¾ cup caramel-flavored topping
1⅛ cups semisweet chocolate chips
1½ teaspoons shortening

1. Prepare Chocolate Cups; set aside.

2. Preheat oven to 375°F. Spread pecans on baking sheet. Bake 8 to 10 minutes or until golden brown, stirring frequently. Remove from baking sheet; cool. Chop ¾ cup pecan halves into uniform pieces. Reserve 36 pecan halves.

3. Spoon scant 1 teaspoon caramel topping into each Chocolate Cup. Top each with 1 teaspoon chopped pecans, pressing gently; set aside.

4. Fill bottom pan of double boiler with water to 1 inch below level of top pan. Bring water just to a boil; reduce heat to low. Place chocolate chips and shortening in top of double boiler. Stir until chocolate is melted. Remove from heat.

5. Spoon scant 1 teaspoon melted chocolate around perimeter of each cup; smooth toward center until cup is fully covered. Immediately place one toasted pecan half in center. Let stand in cool place until firm. Store at room temperature in airtight container.

Makes 36 candy cups

Almond Butter Crunch

1 cup BLUE DIAMOND® Blanched Slivered Almonds
½ cup butter
½ cup sugar
1 tablespoon light corn syrup

Line bottom and side of 8- or 9-inch cake pan with aluminum foil (not plastic wrap or wax paper). Butter foil heavily; set aside. Combine almonds, butter, sugar and corn syrup in 10-inch skillet. Bring to a boil over medium heat, stirring constantly. Boil, stirring constantly, until mixture turns golden brown, about 5 to 6 minutes. Working quickly, spread candy in prepared pan. Cool about 15 minutes or until firm. Remove candy from pan by lifting edges of foil. Peel off foil. Cool thoroughly. Break into pieces.

Makes about ¾ pound

Fudgy Banana Rocky Road Clusters

1 package (12 ounces) semisweet chocolate chips (2 cups)
⅓ cup peanut butter
3 cups miniature marshmallows
1 cup unsalted peanuts
1 cup banana chips

Line baking sheets with waxed paper. Grease waxed paper.

Place chocolate chips and peanut butter in large microwavable bowl. Microwave at HIGH 2 minutes or until chips are melted and mixture is smooth, stirring twice. Fold in marshmallows, peanuts and banana chips.

Drop rounded tablespoonfuls candy mixture onto prepared baking sheets; refrigerate until firm. Store in airtight container in refrigerator.

Makes 2½ to 3 dozen clusters

Tip: If you prefer more nuts, use chunky peanut butter.

Raspberry Truffles

2 cups (12 ounces) semisweet chocolate chips
¾ cup sweetened condensed milk
¼ cup seedless raspberry jam
2 tablespoons butter or margarine
1 tablespoon framboise (raspberry brandy)
3 ounces white chocolate, coarsely chopped

1. Melt chips with condensed milk, jam and butter in heavy, medium saucepan over low heat, stirring occasionally. Whisk in brandy until blended. Pour into pie pan. Refrigerate until mixture is fudgy but soft, about 1½ hours. Line baking sheet with waxed paper; set aside.

2. Melt white chocolate in bowl over hot, not boiling water, stirring constantly.

3. Shape about 1 tablespoonful of mixture into 1¼-inch ball. To shape, roll mixture in your palms. Repeat with remaining mixture; place truffles on prepared baking sheet.

4. Spoon melted white chocolate over top one third of each truffle. Refrigerate until chocolate is firm.

5. Remove from waxed paper; place in miniature paper candy cups. Truffles can be refrigerated 2 to 3 days or frozen several weeks.

Makes about 40 truffles

Double-Chocolate Coffee Balls

1 can (8 ounces) almond paste
3 tablespoons bourbon
1 egg white
3 cups powdered sugar, divided
54 to 56 purchased chocolate-coated coffee beans
16 ounces premium semisweet or bittersweet chocolate, chopped
⅔ cup heavy cream

1. Beat almond paste, bourbon and egg white in medium bowl with electric mixer at medium speed until blended. Add 2 cups powdered sugar; beat at low speed until well mixed. Place on surface dusted with powdered sugar. Knead in remaining 1 cup powdered sugar until smooth. Shape into two 1¼-inch diameter logs. Cut one ¼-inch slice from log. Flatten slightly into circle. Sprinkle work surface with powdered sugar as needed to prevent sticking. Keep logs covered with plastic wrap until ready to cut.

2. Place coffee bean in center of slice; fold sides up around coffee bean. With fingertips, smooth into ball. Set on tray lined with waxed paper. Cover lightly with plastic wrap. Repeat steps with remaining log until all balls are made. Place balls in freezer.

3. Fill bottom pan of double boiler with water to 1 inch below level of top pan. Bring water just to a boil; reduce heat to low. Place chocolate in top of double boiler. Stir until chocolate is melted. While chocolate is melting, bring heavy cream to a boil over medium-high heat in small saucepan. Remove from heat. Add hot cream all at once to melted chocolate; whisk quickly until mixture is smooth and glossy (the initial graininess will disperse). Check temperature of chocolate with candy thermometer and maintain between 125° to 130°F while dipping.

4. Remove tray from freezer. Dip balls in melted chocolate with dipping fork or spoon, tapping handle a few times against side of pan to allow excess chocolate to drain back into pan. Remove excess chocolate by scraping bottom of ball across rim of saucepan. Place balls back on waxed paper. Let stand in cool place 20 minutes; refrigerate 1 hour. Gently remove balls from waxed paper and place in small baking cups. Store in airtight container in freezer or refrigerator.

Makes about 4½ dozen candies

Chocolate Mint Squares

6 tablespoons butter (no substitutes)
½ cup HERSHEY'S Cocoa
2 cups powdered sugar
3 tablespoons plus 1 teaspoon milk, divided
1 teaspoon vanilla extract
Mint Filling (recipe follows)

1. Line 8-inch square pan with foil, extending foil over edges of pan.

2. Melt butter in small saucepan over low heat; add cocoa. Cook, stirring constantly, just until mixture is smooth. Remove from heat; add powdered sugar, 3 tablespoons milk and vanilla. Cook over low heat, stirring constantly, until mixture is glossy. Spread half of mixture into prepared pan. Refrigerate.

3. Meanwhile, prepare Mint Filling; spread filling over chocolate layer. Refrigerate 10 minutes.

4. To remaining chocolate mixture in saucepan, add remaining 1 teaspoon milk. Cook over low heat, stirring constantly, until smooth. Spread quickly over filling. Refrigerate until firm. Use foil to lift candy out of pan; peel off foil. Cut candy into squares. Store in tightly covered container in refrigerator.

Makes about 4 dozen pieces

Mint Filling

1 package (3 ounces) cream cheese, softened
2 cups powdered sugar
½ teaspoon vanilla extract
¼ teaspoon peppermint extract
3 to 5 drops green food color
Milk

Beat cream cheese, powdered sugar, vanilla, peppermint extract and food color in small bowl until smooth. Add 2 to 3 teaspoons milk, if needed, for spreading consistency.

ACKNOWLEDGMENTS

The publisher would like to thank the companies and organizations listed below for the use of their recipes and photographs in this publication.

Blue Diamond Growers®

Del Monte Corporation

Duncan Hines® and Moist Deluxe® are registered trademarks of Aurora Foods Inc.

Eagle® Brand

Equal® sweetener

Hershey Foods Corporation

© Mars, Incorporated 2002

McIlhenny Company (TABASCO® brand Pepper Sauce)

National Honey Board

National Sunflower Association

Nestlé USA

The Quaker® Oatmeal Kitchens

Reckitt Benckiser Inc.

Southeast United Dairy Industry Association, Inc.

Washington Apple Commission

INDEX

METRIC CONVERSION CHART

VOLUME MEASUREMENTS (dry)

$1/8$ teaspoon = 0.5 mL
$1/4$ teaspoon = 1 mL
$1/2$ teaspoon = 2 mL
$3/4$ teaspoon = 4 mL
1 teaspoon = 5 mL
1 tablespoon = 15 mL
2 tablespoons = 30 mL
$1/4$ cup = 60 mL
$1/3$ cup = 75 mL
$1/2$ cup = 125 mL
$2/3$ cup = 150 mL
$3/4$ cup = 175 mL
1 cup = 250 mL
2 cups = 1 pint = 500 mL
3 cups = 750 mL
4 cups = 1 quart = 1 L

VOLUME MEASUREMENTS (fluid)

1 fluid ounce (2 tablespoons) = 30 mL
4 fluid ounces ($1/2$ cup) = 125 mL
8 fluid ounces (1 cup) = 250 mL
12 fluid ounces ($1 1/2$ cups) = 375 mL
16 fluid ounces (2 cups) = 500 mL

WEIGHTS (mass)

$1/2$ ounce = 15 g
1 ounce = 30 g
3 ounces = 90 g
4 ounces = 120 g
8 ounces = 225 g
10 ounces = 285 g
12 ounces = 360 g
16 ounces = 1 pound = 450 g

DIMENSIONS

$1/16$ inch = 2 mm
$1/8$ inch = 3 mm
$1/4$ inch = 6 mm
$1/2$ inch = 1.5 cm
$3/4$ inch = 2 cm
1 inch = 2.5 cm

OVEN TEMPERATURES

250°F = 120°C
275°F = 140°C
300°F = 150°C
325°F = 160°C
350°F = 180°C
375°F = 190°C
400°F = 200°C
425°F = 220°C
450°F = 230°C

BAKING PAN SIZES

Utensil	Size in Inches/Quarts	Metric Volume	Size in Centimeters
Baking or Cake Pan (square or rectangular)	8×8×2	2 L	20×20×5
	9×9×2	2.5 L	23×23×5
	12×8×2	3 L	30×20×5
	13×9×2	3.5 L	33×23×5
Loaf Pan	8×4×3	1.5 L	20×10×7
	9×5×3	2 L	23×13×7
Round Layer Cake Pan	8×1½	1.2 L	20×4
	9×1½	1.5 L	23×4
Pie Plate	8×1¼	750 mL	20×3
	9×1¼	1 L	23×3
Baking Dish or Casserole	1 quart	1 L	—
	1½ quart	1.5 L	—
	2 quart	2 L	—